LET US GO ON

Studies in Hebrews 5 and 6

A Handbook for Disciples

Also by David Lillie

BEYOND CHARISMA

LET US GO ON
Studies in Hebrews 5 and 6

A Handbook for Disciples

by David Lillie

The Paternoster Press

Copyright © 1991 David Lillie

All rights reserved. No part of this publication may be reproduced, stored in a retrieval system, or transmitted in any form or by any means, electronic, mechanical, photocopying, recording or otherwise, without the prior permission of the publisher or a licence permitting restricted copying. In the U.K. such licences are issued by the Copyright Licensing Agency, 90 Tottenham Court Road, London, W1P 9HE.

AUSTRALIA:
Bookhouse Australia Ltd.,
P.O. Box 115, Flemington Markets, NSW 2129

British Library Cataloguing in Publication Data

Lillie, David
   Let us go on: studies in the Epistle to the Hebrews chapters 5 and 6.
   1. Christianity. Scriptures. Bible. N. T. Hebrews
   I. Title
   227.8706

ISBN 0–85364–519–1

Typeset by Photoprint, Torquay, Devon
and printed and bound in Great Britain for The Paternoster Press,
Paternoster House, 3 Mount Radford Crescent, Exeter, Devon
by BPCC Wheatons Ltd., Exeter.

Contents

Foreword	vii
1 The Great Salvation	1
2 The Exhortation (1)	10
3 The Exhortation (2)	20
4 The Exhortation (3)	34
5 Background to the Warning of Apostasy (Hebrews 6:4–8)	48
6 The Warning of Apostasy	59
7 Strong Encouragement	75
Postscript: Crisis in Grace Community Church	83

Foreword

THIS STUDY IS BASED MAINLY ON HEBREWS, CHAPTERS 5 and 6, at the heart of which is to be found one of the most "difficult" passages in the New Testament.

It has not been my intention to attempt a detailed exposition of these chapters. But as one who has sought over many years to listen to the voice of the Holy Spirit, I have attempted here to pass on certain insights with which I have been personally challenged, and which I believe to be of the utmost importance to God's people today.

My book may be likened to a small fishing vessel whose registration number is "HEB 5–6" and which may often be seen pursuing its business in home waters. But, as need arises, it is taken, from time to time, into neighbouring waters, or even into more distant areas where the harvest of the sea is plentiful.

For the fulfilment of my task, therefore, I have made numerous excursions, even beyond the limits of the epistle, into neighbouring and also more distant parts of God's Word in pursuit of the business of the 'Master Fisherman'. Always, however, it will be seen that we return eventually to the port from which we originally set sail. This, I hope, will give a greater measure of coherence and credibility to my message.

The epistle to the Hebrews as a whole, and chapters 5 and 6 in particular, encapsulates perhaps the most neglected element in the "neglected" gospel—"The Gospel of the Kingdom". I refer to the revelation concerning Sonship, and the Inheritance, and, in that connection, the vital importance of the high priestly ministry of the Lord Jesus.

I wish to acknowledge here my indebtedness to my wife Kathleen, and to several friends who have read these chapters and whose comments have been very helpful to me in the editorial process. Especially I would record my indebtedness to the late Mr George Lang whose exposition of "Hebrews", and other writings, have been for me, through many years, a great inspiration and encouragement.

The "parabolic fantasy" which I have included as a "postscript" at the end of the book was written originally to serve a particular purpose. It has been included in this volume because it seems relevant to the main study and may help to clarify for some readers why the warnings as well as the encouragements of "our gospel" are needed so greatly today among the Lord's people.

My burden in writing these chapters has been to make some contribution towards a greater understanding of "the whole counsel of God" among his people in these challenging times.

All scripture quotations (unless otherwise stated) are from the Revised Standard Version (1952).

EXETER, Spring 1991. DAVID LILLIE

Chapter One

The Great Salvation

THE CENTRAL THEME OF THE HEBREW EPISTLE IS THE HIGH priestly ministry of the Lord Jesus.

In developing this theme (in chapter five) the writer quotes from one of the great messianic psalms so treasured by the Jews because of the hope these psalms provided that, even after centuries of weary waiting, their promised Messiah would yet come.

Psalm 110 begins with the striking statement: "The LORD says to my lord: 'Sit at my right hand till I make your enemies your footstool.'" A little later come the words which our writer quotes: "The LORD has sworn, and will not change his mind, 'You are a priest for ever after the order of Melchizedek.'"

Apart from the fact that Melchizedek was the king of Salem, little is known about this mysterious Old Testament personage. But, as the writer asserts, he must have been very great since even the patriach Abraham gave him a tithe of all his spoils. Linking this prophetic statement about Melchizedek with Jesus, our writer now proceeds to unfold the profound significance of this revelation.

Note how he leads into his theme. Hebrews 5:7–10, contains one of the most profound and moving statements in Scripture. We should consider these verses carefully at this point, as they introduce and set the standard for what is to follow:

> In the days of his flesh, Jesus offered up prayers and supplications, with loud cries and tears, to him who was able to save him from death, and he was heard for his godly fear. Although he was a Son, he learned obedience through what he suffered; and being made perfect he became the source of eternal salvation to all who obey him, being designated by God a priest after the order of Melchizedek.

As the people to whom this epistle was originally addressed

were Jews, they would have been well instructed in their national history and religion, and have had access to what was known about Melchizedek. They also confessed Jesus as their Messiah and Lord. And since, in the psalm, someone to whom the title "lord" is given is addressed by "The LORD (Jehovah)", and is said to be "a priest for ever after the order of Melchizedek", it is the burden on the writer's heart to explain how that prophetic reference has found fulfilment in the person and ministry of Jesus.

But he hesitates. "About this," he says, "we have much to say which is hard to explain." Are these brethren ready to receive this further revelation? He evidently knows certain things about them which are not too reassuring. So, before continuing with his theme, he turns aside to give them some words of exhortation and warning.

It is to this passage in parenthesis that we shall be giving particular attention in these studies. But first, some comments are called for with reference to the epistle as a whole.

Although most Christians are not of Jewish (or Hebrew) origin, and have a different religious and ethnic background, it should not be assumed that some parts of this "Hebrew" epistle are not therefore applicable to non-Jewish Christians. Hebrews forms an integral part of the New Testament, which, in its entirety, is the Christian's charter. In fact, it is in Hebrews alone that we find any exposition of the themes of "the New Covenant (or Testament)", or of the high priestly ministry of Jesus. If we value that ministry, then we should note that alongside this exposition, there are five challenging "warning passages".

These warnings seem to present difficulties to some expositors. Confidently asserting that the high priestly ministry of Jesus applies to the Christian, when they come to the warnings, they apply these to an imaginary community of Jewish "professors" of Christ, who are alleged not to be true "born again" believers. This is, however, a regrettable mishandling of the Word of God. In Hebrews, the high priestly ministry of Jesus and the warnings, are inseparable; we cannot claim the one and ignore the other. This epistle belongs to all the Lord's people throughout this age, regardless of race.

The Great Salvation 3

If confirmation of this is needed, we might turn to an important passage in 1 Corinthians chapter ten. Here, drawing attention to the consequences of the disobedience of the children of Israel during their journey through the wilderness to the Promised Land, Paul says (verse 11): "Now these things happened to them as a warning, but they were written down for our instruction, upon whom the end of the ages has come."

Paul is writing here to a church which is predominantly non-Jewish, yet what he is saying to them accords entirely with the message of Hebrews. Paul is, in fact, simply being a faithful teacher of the Gospel of the Kingdom which the Lord preached, and which he commissioned his disciples to take to the nations.

This fact needs to be thoroughly grasped. So much "gospel preaching" or "Bible teaching" either skirts around this important component of the New Testament, or, by implication, dismisses it altogether. Could this be a major reason for the appalling casualty rate among professed converts to the Christian faith, and of backsliding generally among what are known as "Evangelicals" (including many who claim to be "Pentecostals" or "Charismatics")? In my own Christian background, reference was often made to what was called "the simple gospel". For years I myself endeavoured to preach such a gospel. Attention was focused on such scriptures as Ephesians 2:8: "For by grace you have been saved through faith; and this is not of your own doing, it is the gift of God—not because of works, lest any man should boast;" and on John 3:16, which was sometimes referred to as "the gospel in a nutshell".

John 3:16 contains a precious truth which I can say I rejoice in today more than ever. But such verses, taken, as they so often are, out of the context of the whole counsel of God, present only one important ingredient of the New Testament gospel. They focus attention on what God has done in Christ to save me from eternal loss, and on the basis of faith in Christ alone, offer me the assurance of eternal life. This is wonderful news indeed. But it is not the whole of the gospel which Jesus preached, and which he commissioned his disciples to preach to the nations.

It should also be confessed that, although the language of triumph might often be on my lips, that "simple gospel" failed to provide an adequate incentive to live a holy and purposeful life for God. It was a marvellously secure foundation on which to build one's life, but since it was all "by grace through faith (and) not of works," where was the challenge? In my heart there was a nagging sense that there was a further dimension of spiritual truth into which I had not yet entered. Then came the discovery of the truth of the Kingdom. I was, of course, familiar with the New Testament references to "the kingdom of God" but I had been led to assume that these references applied to the Jews. As regards the references to the heavenly calling, and to reigning with Christ, I had assumed that they were part of the package of salvation secured for all "saved" Christians on the basis of "simple faith" alone.

What an incentive for holy living it was to discover that I was called to be involved, even in this life, in the service of Christ, the designated King of the earth! What a challenge it has continued to be to see from God's Word that those who are to reign with Christ are those who have served him faithfully, who have suffered with him and for him; those who have not been overcome by the evil one, but have earned the right to be included in the noble order of overcomers referred to in the letters to the seven churches in Revelation, chapters 2 and 3! Whilst it may not be easy to understand the symbolic language in which some of those letters are couched, two of them—those addressed to the overcomers in Thyatira and Laodicea—are clear enough.

To the overcomers in the church at Thyatira the designated king writes: "He who conquers and keeps my words until the end, I will give him power over the nations, and he shall rule them with a rod of iron, as when earthen pots are broken in pieces, even as I myself have received power from my Father . . ." (Revelation 2:26,27).

Similarly, to the overcomers in the church at Laodicea, he says: "He who conquers, I will grant him to sit with me on my throne, as I myself conquered and sat down with my Father on his throne. He who has an ear, let him hear what the Spirit says to the churches" (3:21,22).

The Great Salvation

The offer of forgiveness of sin on the basis of faith in the Lord Jesus Christ is indeed a fundamental part of the gospel. But it is not the whole gospel. When earlier this writer challenges his readers with the question: "How shall we escape if we neglect such a great salvation?" (2:3) he is challenging men and women who have already come to faith in Christ in response to the preaching of the Gospel of the Kingdom. They knew, what all of us should know, that the "great salvation" referred to is something much more than forgiveness and justification and regeneration, wonderful though those blessings are.

A man falls down a pit, and cries for help until somebody hears him and lets down a rope to him. Eagerly he grasps the rope and clings to it whilst he is hauled to safety. Now he has other requirements: dry clothes, a warm meal, some medical attention, maybe, and, hopefully, the comforts of home and family once more.

Whilst still down the pit, the prospect of "home and family" may have looked to him the ultimate of bliss; in reality, after a day or two, they may be found to fall far short of that. We live in a world which is full of disappointed, disillusioned people, including many who are professed followers of Christ. Jesus said: "A man's life does not consist in the abundance of his possessions"; not even in the comforts of the home.

What then is the missing dimension in that foundational gospel? In one word, it is "purpose". But can this be true in the lives of people who know the Lord Jesus as their Saviour? It would seem so. The psalmist testified: "He brought me out of a horrible pit, and out of the miry clay, and set my feet upon a rock, and put a new song in my mouth."

That is a wonderful testimony to the grace of God. From God's viewpoint, however, it is not the ultimate in the salvation he has designed for his people. We used to have a tract with the title: "Safety, Certainty and Enjoyment", which was widely used in bringing people to faith in Christ. But a moment's reflection will suffice to recognize that "safety, certainty and enjoyment" do no more than sum up what fallen, self-centred man wants for himself. The focus is entirely man-centred.

Safety, certainty and enjoyment are tremendous blessings which we all covet, and since we are all naturally self-centred it may well be that these are the only inducements which would attract most of us initially to the Saviour. But unless these blessing are harnessed to divine "purpose" they fail to constitute the "great salvation" to which our writer refers in Hebrews 2. In that chapter (verse 10) we read: "It was fitting that he, for whom and by whom all things exist, in bringing many sons to glory, should make the pioneer of their salvation perfect through suffering." There, in brief, we have the divine purpose for which the Son of God came into the world: "to bring many sons to glory".

To understand this, we need to go back to the beginning of man's history. In Genesis 1:26ff we read: "Then God said, 'Let us make man in our image, after our likeness'." It may be hard to grasp the fact that our human race was made in the image of God. It is harder still, perhaps, to realize that God has never given up on man, and will not rest until he has around him a family of human origin who are fitted and qualified to fulfil his original purpose in creating man. Yet the "great salvation" of Hebrews is nothing less than that. God's purpose in the gospel is the restoration of manhood to the place of glory and honour which he designed for man originally.

What we wanted from God when we found ourselves down in the pit with our feet deep in the mire was to be rescued, reclothed, fed, and provided for. But God had a much more ambitious plan than that for us. It was that we might become "sons" (and "daughters") like his uniquely wonderful Son. That was why that Son—"the Beloved One"—came to this earth, and himself became a man, taking the human name of Jesus. That is why Jesus went to the cross as the sin-bearer and sin-purger. It was, as the verse we have just quoted says, for the purpose of "bringing many sons to glory" that he, "for whom and by whom all things exist", was "made perfect through suffering".

Does that imply that he had previously been "imperfect"? Most certainly not. He was the one of whom the Father declared: "This is my beloved Son in whom are all my delights."

He had, however, a purpose which could not be fulfilled (or "perfected") other than by the laying down of his sinless, human life. "I have a baptism to be baptized with" he told his disciples, referring to his death; "and how I am constrained ('held in', or 'compressed') until it is accomplished!" Perfect in character and in his obedience to the Father in all that he did, at that point in time, he was "imperfect" only in the sense that the great work he had come to do had not yet been accomplished. But there came the moment when as he hung on the cross he gave up his spirit and cried in triumph: "Finished", or "accomplished"; (one word only in the original Greek).

It is *sons* the Father seeks. When in the parable, the prodigal resolved to return to the father, all he hoped for, all he actually wanted, was the security and the amenities of a comfortable and liberal household. "Make me one of your hired servants," was the request he had resolved to make to his father. His father, however, had different plans. Nothing less than restoration to full sonship for his lost boy would satisfy him. From God's viewpoint, that is the meaning of "salvation". God seeks "sons" conformed to the image of his dear Son. To obtain such sons he was willing to pay the ultimate price.

Here is the great wonder. So completely were Father and Son at one in that great purpose that, to pay that price, the Son went to the cross and died in agony and shame at the hands of sinful men. Luke tells us that his face was set to go to Jerusalem knowing perfectly the death that awaited him there. Our writer says that it was "for the joy that was set before him (that he) endured the cross, despising the shame". It is because of that that he is now "seated at the right hand of the throne of God" (Luke 9:51; Hebrews 12:2).

In Hebrews, we enter a dimension of "salvation truth" reaching far beyond the basic dimension which focuses on the grace of God meeting the sinner's need of forgiveness. God seeks *SONS*. Of *THE* Son the writer tells us: "He learned obedience through what he suffered; and being made perfect he became the source of eternal salvation to all who obey him" (5:8).

Later, the writer says confidently: "In your case, beloved,

we feel sure of better things that belong to salvation". Better things, that is, than were the consequence of Israel's rebellion against Moses (and God) at Kadesh-Barnea, on which tragic story he had based the solemn warning just previously given. And it is from that confident assertion that he moves on to say: "And we desire each one of you to show the same earnestness in realizing the full assurance of hope until the end, so that you may not be sluggish, but imitators of those who through faith and patience inherit the promise" (6:11).

"Things which belong to salvation"—in the context of this passage—can mean only things that belong to the working out of the divine purpose in the creation of a glorious new family of "sons". The salvation we are to strive for is the attainment of "sonship". Only those attain to this who partake of the spirit of "the Son" who, as the pioneer of their salvation, was "made perfect through suffering". It is thus that Jesus became the source (or pioneer) of eternal salvation to all who obey him. It is "sons" (and daughters!) who are to share the throne of his glory.

Who among us can hope to attain this? In our own strength, not one. That is why, in this epistle, the exhortations and warnings are inseparably linked with the high priestly ministry of Jesus, and why such emphasis is given to his having become "a priest for ever after the order of Melchizedek"—an eternal, unchanging priesthood, which is in no way subject, like the Aaronic priesthood, to human weakness.

Time and again in Hebrews these fearful and slothful believers are taken back to the ever present reality of that ministry. Without Jesus as the Lamb of God who shed his blood for us, we would be eternally lost. Without our great High Priest who ever lives to plead for us before the throne of his Father, though saved and forgiven, we would utterly fail to live the overcoming life, and consequently fail to claim our inheritance. But with Jesus as our Saviour and as our High Priest to sustain us in the day to day conflict, we have all that we need to enable us to "go on to maturity" and to "sonship"—and to the eternal inheritance.

Isaac Watts, in one of his hymns, captures the spirit of

adventure and ambition which the risen Lord Jesus looks for in those who aspire to that great purpose:

Then let my soul arise, and tread the tempter down;
My Captain leads me forth to conquest and a crown.
The feeblest saint shall win the day
Though death and hell obstruct the way. Amen!

Chapter Two

The Exhortation (1)

IN DEVELOPING THE THEME OF THE HIGH PRIESTLY MINISTRY of Jesus, the Son of God, the writer says that this is "after the order of Melchizedek".

"About this," he tells them, "we have much to say which is hard to explain, since you have become dull of hearing. For though by this time you ought to be teachers, you need someone to teach you again the first principles of God's word. You need milk, not solid food; for everyone who lives on milk is unskilled in the word of righteousness, for he is a child. But solid food is for the mature, for those who have their faculties trained by practice to distinguish good from evil."

In this exhortation there is no suggestion that the people addressed are dim-witted, incapable of understanding the deep truths the writer wants to share with them. Their dullness is spiritual; and what particularly concerns him is that this had not always been the case with them. They have *become* dull of hearing.

This is made clear when later (in chapter 10) he reminds them of the former days when, after they were enlightened, they endured much suffering and abuse, even taking joyfully the plundering of their property, since they knew that there was awaiting them "a better possession and an abiding one". Now, it seems, they have lost much of their early zeal and spiritual awareness.

Their condition is similar to that of their forefathers at the time when the Lord sent Jeremiah to speak to them. In Jeremiah 2:2 we read:

> Thus says the LORD,
> I remember the devotion of your youth,
>   your love as a bride,
> how you followed me in the wilderness,
>   in a land not sown.

The Exhortation (1)

> Israel was holy to the LORD,
> the first fruits of his harvest.

Then later (verse 7):

> And I brought you into a plentiful land
> to enjoy its fruits and its good things.
> But when you came in you defiled my land,
> and made my heritage an abomination.

And (verse 13):

> My people have committed two evils:
> they have forsaken me,
> the fountain of living waters,
> and hewed out cisterns for themselves,
> broken cisterns, that can hold no water.

We can sense here the Lord's sorrow as he reproaches his people for their betrayal of his love. How much greater must be his sorrow when those who have been redeemed under the terms of the New Covenant cease to hear him, and turn away from him!

These Hebrew Christians had become dull of hearing. The evidence given for this is that "though by this time you ought to be teachers, you need someone to teach you again the first principles of God's word."

In Ephesians 4 Paul says that the ascended Lord "gave some the gift of teaching," and in 1 Corinthians 12, he asks: "Are all teachers?" with the obvious implication that the correct answer is "No". Is our writer being fair then when he addresses these friends as a group, and says: "By this time you ought to be teachers", if, in fact, teaching is a special gift given only to the few? Undoubtedly, in Ephesians 4 and 1 Corinthians 12, Paul is talking about a special gift of teaching in the sense of expounding, or explaining, the Word of God. This is certainly not given to all, nor, it should be said, is it acquired overnight in one mighty spiritual visitation.

What the writer has in mind here is the much broader aspect of teaching which is the communication of knowledge and experience. Such teaching can be deliberate, or it can be quite spontaneous, and even unconscious. When, for example, we say of someone that he (or she) is a living testimony for Christ, or we speak of the lessons we have learned from someone's life, we are talking about communication—or teaching—which is often quite unconscious.

A child will take a younger brother or sister by the hand and teach it to toddle, or hold a spoon. Often young girls develop what we call "the maternal instinct". Such examples can be found right across the spectrum of human and animal life. They illustrate important aspects of a God-given ability to communicate what we ourselves have been taught. That basically is what teaching is. Such abilities are often developed most successfully in people who couldn't win a teacher's diploma to save their lives!

The same principles apply on the spiritual level, but with an important difference. In this connection, the first two chapters of Paul's first epistle to the Corinthians are very helpful.

Here is a passage from chapter 2:11–13:

> For what person knows a man's thoughts except the spirit of the man which is in him? So also no one comprehends the thoughts of God except the Spirit of God. Now we have received not the spirit of the world, but the Spirit which is from God, that we might understand the gifts bestowed on us by God. And we impart this in words not taught by human wisdom but taught by the Spirit, interpreting spiritual truths to those who possess the Spirit.

The primacy of the Spirit in these verses is to be noted. The ministry of the Spirit is of an entirely different order, or "dimension", from "natural" ministry. The Holy Spirit sends the most brilliant intellectual, and the most gifted orator, back to the classroom to sit alongside those referred to by Paul earlier as being, by worldly standards, "foolish, weak, low and despised".

It is there, with hearts open to the Lord, that the thoughts of God are communicated to us by his Spirit. It is there that, by his grace, we may receive his gifting, not all in one package, nor necessarily with a special label such as "teacher", "prophet", "caster out of demons", or "evangelist", attached. Rather, it is "here a little and there a little" that

The Exhortation (1)

we receive ability to communicate what has first been made living and meaningful to us by the Holy Spirit. That, in essence, is the ministry of teaching in the broader sense to which our writer is here referring. And the sad thing about these Christians to whom he is writing is that as channels of communication of divine truth they are no longer in working order. They have become dull of hearing. There is no outflow because there is no intake.

The risen Lord had promised his disciples that at Pentecost: "You shall receive power when the Holy Spirit has come upon you; and you shall be my witnesses" (Acts 1:8). That promise was to all the disciples, including the women who are specifically mentioned in this connection. The order of events is, first instruction (Luke tells us in Acts 1 that, after his resurrection, Jesus took his apostles aside and taught them concerning the Kingdom of God); then revelation, when the Holy Spirit makes livingly real to our hearts what we have learned; and then communication.

Instruction, revelation, communication. Some of the disciples emerged later as people with a recognized teaching gift; but all without exception were to share the privilege of communicating what they had received from the Lord. Hence in the broader and important sense, all would be involved in the ministry of teaching.

What we are considering is the law of life operating within the community of God's Spirit-born New Covenant people—"the natural law in the spiritual world". In 1 Corinthians 2 Paul emphasizes the fact that, in spiritual ministry, the Spirit-born servant of the Lord receives, first of all, revelation by the Holy Spirit. Then he is anointed to be an interpreter of what he has received "to those who possess the Spirit"—that is, to those who are also prepared by the Spirit to receive the word. This does not rule out natural ability, but it emphasizes that it is the Holy Spirit who is essentially the teacher. Hence Paul stresses the importance of our dependence as ministers (and all Spirit-born Christians should be ministers) on the Holy Spirit.

This would seem to prohibit any who have been called to a teaching ministry from relying on a stock-in-trade of good sermons or messages; or even, should they be blessed with a good memory, on their ability to string together some good bible-based thoughts well embellished by interesting illustrations and spiced with some nice touches of humour. There is nothing wrong with any of these things in their place. But authentic spiritual ministry, such as is envisaged in 1 Corinthians 2, must be of the kind which has first been ministered to the speaker's heart by the Holy Spirit, and is then ministered to others by the Holy Spirit's authority and anointing. However much, or little, we may be in demand as speakers, let us determine that we never become mere preaching machines. To be a communicator of divine truth is a very great privilege. Let us wait on the Lord so that we may become channels through which the living water is poured out for the blessing of those to whom he may send us. "Lord, speak to me that I may speak, in living echoes of thy tone".

We have examined this subject of teaching at some length, but it should perhaps be admitted that the reference to teaching is only incidental to the emphasis which the writer is making in the verse we have been considering (verse 12). He is pointing out that, far from being teachers, these Hebrew Christians needed to be taught again "the first principles of God's word". So it is with their spiritual immaturity that he is primarily concerned. He implies that their understanding of "first principles", or "foundational truths", was still patchy, so that their spiritual infancy has been unduly prolonged. They are still needing milk when by now they should be feeding on solid food.

But what does he mean by "the first principles of God's word?" An important feature of Hebrews is the way it reveals that these "first principles" are rooted, even for New Covenant saints, in Old Testament history and law. Without an understanding of this, much of the New Testament is inexplicable, including the main theme of this epistle—the high priestly ministry of Jesus. To get some grasp of the importance, from God's viewpoint, of those principles, we should look at an Old Testament scripture, Deuteronomy chapter 11:18ff:

> You shall therefore lay up these words of mine in your heart and in your soul; and you shall bind them as a sign upon your

The Exhortation (1)

hand, and they shall be as frontlets between your eyes. And you shall teach them to your children, talking of them when you are sitting in your house, and when you are walking by the way, and when you lie down, and when you rise. And you shall write them upon the doorposts of your house and upon your gates, that your days and the days of your children may be multiplied in the land which the LORD swore to your fathers to give them . . . . For if you will be careful to do all . . . which I command you to do, loving the LORD your God, walking in all his ways, and cleaving to him, then the LORD will drive out all these nations before you . . . . Every place on which the sole of your foot treads shall be yours . . . . No man shall be able to stand against you.

These "first principles" given by the Lord to Old Covenant saints spoke of peace and prosperity, on conditions. How should we interpret them in the context of living today in our affluent "western" society, or should we dismiss them as being no longer relevant, on the basis that "we are not under law, but under grace"?

Such a dismissal would obviously have been wholly unacceptable to this writer to the Hebrew Christians. What is more, it would have been a denial of much of the Lord's teaching in the gospels, and of that of other New Testament writers.

In the Deuteronomy passage, we see that the Lord urged on the people of the Old Covenant the need for their continuous attention to his word. This applied equally to the children of the New Covenant. They were to be a nation whose thinking was conditioned by what our writer refers to (in chapter 6) as "the goodness of the word of God". Their lives were to be subject to a discipline which to some of us living in these days may seem barely tolerable.

But was it so intolerable when we consider what the God of Israel promised? Their homeland was to be a land of plenty, a land of fruitfulness, a land flowing with milk and honey. That does not sound like a dreary, treadmill sort of existence. On the contrary, an acceptance of the discipline of obedience to God's word was the guarantee of an overcoming life of peace and prosperity.

It is this prospect which really underlies the whole message of Hebrews. God's New Covenant people are heirs to what Paul in Ephesians 5:5 refers to as "an inheritance in the kingdom of Christ and of God". The concern of this writer is lest they should fail, like their ancestors, to enter into their inheritance through disobedience. Already they had been warned about this in chapters 3 and 4. They are warned again in the passage immediately following this exhortation, and altogether there are five such warnings in this epistle. In the Ephesians 5 passage just referred to, Paul speaks equally emphatically about the danger of disinheritance through disobedience.

Yet the identification of these Hebrew Christians as born again believers in Christ is never in question. "You need milk" are not words that could apply to stillborn babes, but to live children. But that is all these Christians are; mere children or babes (spiritually speaking), capable only of feeding upon milk when by now they should be feeding on the solid food of the word of righteousness. They are not growing up to "sonship"; they are not developing into the kind of mature, responsible, dependable disciples of Jesus who are proving their fitness to be co-heirs and co-reigners with him in his kingdom. The writer clearly has this in mind when, in the next chapter, he says (6:11,12): "And we desire each one of you to show the same earnestness in realizing the full assurance of hope until the end, so that you may not be sluggish, but imitators of those who through faith and patience inherit the promises." As under the Old Covenant, so under the New, full participation in the inheritance of the kingdom is conditional upon the obedience of faith.

Hebrews 5:13: "For every one who lives on milk is unskilled in the word of righteousness, for he is a child." The Greek word *aperios*, translated "unskilled" in the RSV (and, in other translations, "inexperienced") is not found anywhere else in the New Testament. They are "inexperienced" in the sense that through failure to hear the word of the Lord their spiritual growth is retarded. But along with this, and arising out of it, is their lack of skill as teachers of that word. A reasonable inference from what the writer says is that by this time, when they ought to have been able to teach others, they lack the necessary skill for that purpose.

The Exhortation (1)

So what he is talking about is spiritual maturity. How important is this for us today? It is very important, for reasons we shall see in a moment—and all the more so because it is generally unrecognized. It must also be said that the religious ethos in which most Christians live and worship and serve is not conducive to spiritual growth beyond certain very restricted limits. Ministry in many churches never rises above the level of what is here referred to as "the first principles of God's word".

Often it is the system which is largely to blame. When, even in a large congregation, one or two people are set apart as "the ministers", what encouragement does this offer to the other members of the congregation to see themselves as "ministers" or "serving members", which is what the term signifies? Yet, according to Ephesians 4:14, "the work of the ministry" should be a responsibility shared by all members of the body, not just by one or two professionals. In theory, most spiritual leaders recognize this nowadays, and "lay participation" in ministry is looked upon as a desirable objective. It is good to hear of reforms taking place in some congregations in the direction of the breaking down of the clergy/laity dichotomy. Even so, the dead hand of tradition still lies heavily upon the majority of Christian congregations; and is even becoming increasingly evident among some of the new churches which have arisen out of the "charismatic movement".

But none of us can put all the blame on "the system" for our lack of spiritual growth. Every born again believer has a right of personal access to God at the throne of his grace, and no one can deny to us the availablity of the Holy Spirit to teach us personally, even if we have no human teachers to take us on in the word of righteousness. Furthermore, what we have received from the Lord we are responsible to share with others. We do not have to wait until we have been offered a pulpit before we start to do this.

This really brings us back to the three preconditions for effective service mentioned earlier: instruction, revelation, and communication. Some of us have discovered that these preconditions are closely interrelated. Nothing is more stimulating to further prayerful study of the Word of God than sharing with others what we (and they) have already learned by the Holy Spirit. In the words of the wise man in the Book of Proverbs: "One man gives freely, yet grows all the richer; another witholds what he should give, and only suffers want."

That precept is as true in the spiritual as in the natural realm. We have a beautiful example of this in the boy Jesus. Luke tells us that when as a boy of twelve Jesus was taken by his parents to Jerusalem to the Feast of the Passover, they found him in the temple sitting among the doctors both hearing and asking them questions. It would be interesting to know who learned most; Jesus, or the doctors? Already, in spite of his youth, Jesus saw himself as being involved in his Father's "business". He was already, at that young age, "hearing" his Father; and communicating. No wonder Luke is able to tell us: "Jesus increased in wisdom and in stature and in favour with God and man." In the fulnesss of time, he was able to enter upon his divinely accredited ministry declaring: "The Spirit of the Lord is upon me, because he has anointed me to preach good news . . . ." No man might more justifiably have claimed self-sufficiency for his work; yet never did anyone more consistently declare his utter dependency upon his Father for the very words that he spoke, and for the strength and guidance he needed for all that he did. "I can of myself do nothing", was his invariable assertion.

Hebrews 5:14: "But solid food is for the mature, for those who have their faculties trained by practice to distinguish good from evil."

Here we come to the climax of the argument for the need for maturity. The implication is quite clear. The ability to distinguish between good and evil is not intuitive, "native", ability. It is not given to babes, nor even children, however bright and intelligent they may be; nor is it acquired automatically with the passing of the years. It is a product of maturity, and maturity comes through training in the school of Christ.

One of the marks of maturity is a recognition of your own vulnerability; hence the necessity of seeking the counsel of your peers, and especially of those of greater experience. How much more is this necessary for those who are less

The Exhortation (1)

experienced. Over the years I have known of several men whose zeal for God was never in doubt. But they were "loners"; and they fell.

Let those who are comparative novices in the service of Christ, however dedicated and gifted they may be, beware! In the handling of spiritual issues of a serious nature they may, or they may not, be right in some of their judgments. But here in Hebrews we have a spiritual principle which must not be disregarded; the risks are too great.

Solomon was a man endowed with great wisdom, and this is what he says on this subject (Proverbs 11:14): "Where there is no guidance, a people falls; but in an abundance of counselors there is safety." So even the wisest of men saw the necessity of fellowship in handling the needs of frail humanity. Interestingly, he comes back to the theme again in Proverbs 24:6: "By wise counsel you can wage your war, and in the abundance of counselors there is safety".

Here, corporate "kingdom" strategy in the conflict with the enemy is in view. In a later chapter we shall be considering some of the important implications of this aspect of the Hebrews 5/6 passage for us today.

CHAPTER THREE

The Exhortation (2)

FOLLOWING THE EXHORTATION AT THE END OF HEBREWS 5, the writer adds a valuable footnote, parts of which may surprise us:

> Therefore let us leave the elementary doctrine of Christ and go on to maturity, not laying again a foundation of repentance from dead works and faith toward God, with instruction about ablutions, the laying on of hands, the resurrection of the dead, and eternal judgment. And this we will do if God permits (Hebrews 6:1–3).

The first surprise is that opening word "Therefore". We remember that the writer had just been saying that the Christians to whom he was writing appeared capable of receiving only "the milk" of "the first principles of God's word", yet he now introduces the exhortation "to go on to maturity" with this word "therefore".

Is there not more than a hint here that, in spite of the strong words which he had spoken to them, he knew that, if they chose, these Christians were well able to act more responsibly as disciples of Christ?

With this opening word he is challenging them to prove their potential for spiritual growth.

The second surpise is the introduction of that word "us". So these are not the words of a preacher speaking down to his audience from the comfortable immunity of a pulpit. The writer's exhortation is directed as much to himself as to his hearers. This is characteristic of the epistle as a whole. Wherever the sense allows, the writer uses "we" or "us", rather than "you" or "them". Here are the marks of a true servant, and a reminder that in the school of Christ there are no graduates; graduation day is some future day, fixed by the Lord, and known only to him.

The third and biggest surprise is that the writer should exhort his friends to join him in leaving "the elementary

The Exhortation (2)

doctrine of Christ". Why should he do this? Do any of us ever reach a place where we can afford to forget the basics of the faith? We need to give careful thought to this.

First, we should note the obvious connection between "the elementary doctrine of Christ" and the earlier reference to "the first principles of God's word" (5:12). In the writer's mind these both belong to the "milk" category, as compared with the "solid food" of "the word of righteousness", which is the food of the mature.

He is not saying that milk is not good food. Milk continues to be a normal part of most people's diet throughout their lives. (Milk bottles seen outside somebody's back door are no proof that there are children living in that home.) But the point is that, for adults, milk is no longer the main food. Adults should have left the milk stage, and be on to solid food. The trouble with these Hebrew Christians was that they had not done that. In spiritual terms, when by now they ought themselves to be teaching others, they were still needing someone to teach them the first principles of God's Word.

As Hebrews, they had been brought up on those "first principles" even before they had come to Christ, and there is no suggestion that that had not been a very good foundation. "What advantage has the Jew?" Paul asks the Romans. "Much in every way. To begin with, the Jews are entrusted with the oracles of God." Thus they had started with a great advantage. But it had brought its own peculiar problems. This is what is implied in what follows: "Let us go on to maturity, not laying again a foundation of repentance from dead works, and of faith toward God, with instructions about ablutions, the laying on of hands, the resurrection of the dead, and eternal judgment."

All this had been part of "the oracles of God" which had been entrusted to the Jews. It had been the foundation of the religious instruction of these brethren from their youth up. Any teaching which contravened those first principles would have been anathema to them. When first challenged by the claims of Jesus of Nazareth, therefore, they would have needed to be satisfied on several counts before deciding what their response to those claims should be.

As to Jesus's personal character, it could only be acknowledged that they found no fault in him. As to his works, here too, his record was immensely impressive. What then about Jesus's teaching? That, for the Pharisees and Scribes, was the really big test. They eagerly listened to his talk in the hope that they might hear something on which they might take issue with him. But to their dismay, they were unable to fault him even in his teaching.

Jesus emphatically asserted that he had not come to set at naught the law and the prophets; in fact he constantly drew attention to the prophets to attest his own words and works. So loyal was he to the prophets, and so consistent in his life to their moral teaching, that it was on that account (paradoxically) that the religious leaders were so incensed against him. For it was his blameless life and teaching which exposed their own hypocrisy and the way in which, by their traditions, they set the law at naught.

Jesus was a preacher whose message always demanded a verdict. John tells us that, for the majority of the Jews, that verdict was that "they received him not". "Away with him . . . crucify him . . . we will not have this man to reign over us . . ." would have been the majority vote if a referendum had been taken in Jerusalem in Passover Week in the year AD 30, or thereabouts.

We must not therefore underestimate the courage of these men and women who had been willing to stand up among their fellow Hebrews and be counted as disciples of Jesus. This writer had not forgotten those days. In fact, later, in chapter 10, he specifically refers to them when he invites his friends to:

> recall the former days when, after you were enlightened, you endured a hard struggle with sufferings, sometimes being publicly exposed to abuse and affliction, and sometimes being partners with those so treated. For you had compassion on the prisoners, and you joyfully accepted the plundering of your property, since you knew that you yourselves had a better possession and an abiding one.

Their courage had been born out of the overwhelming conviction that Jesus was all he claimed to be. Truly, he was the Son of God, and the promised Messiah! Yet in

The Exhortation (2)

becoming his disciples, they saw no obligation to renounce their God-given national heritage. On the contrary, his claims and teaching only highlighted for them its immense practical implications. Jesus had lifted the oracles of God out of the graveclothes of rabbinical tradition and shown them to be not only foundational, but living and relevant. That was why they had, from the first, set so much store by those "first principles" of the Law. Furthermore, when challenged concerning their commitment to Jesus, it would have been to the Law and the Prophets that they would have turned for justification.

With all these criteria the writer of this epistle identified fully, as evidenced by the fact that he referred to those Old Testament teachings as being "the elementary doctrine of Christ". So what was the problem? Simply that though these friends had come to faith in Jesus as their Messiah, and committed themselves to him as their Saviour and Lord, they had not moved on in all the implications of his kingdom teaching.

Jesus had made it clear right from the beginning that the scope of his messianic mission was not limited to serving the temporal interests of the Jewish people. "Repent for the kingdom of heaven is at hand" was the message with which John the Baptist, and then Jesus himself, had challenged them. Their immediate response had been enthusiastic until Jesus began to spell out the moral implications of his message, and to show that "the kingdom of heaven" would embrace peoples of all nations on the basis of personal faith in, and commitment to, him. It was then that the religious leaders began to oppose him so vigorously.

In his first recorded personal interview, Jesus told Nicodemus that "unless a man is born again he cannot see the kingdom of God"; and his first recorded public discourse—the Sermon on the Mount—begins with the statement "Blessed are the poor in spirit, for theirs is the kingdom of heaven." Matthew tells us that his teaching astonished the crowds, "for he taught as one who had authority, and not as their scribes". Yet throughout his ministry, Jesus authenticated his teaching by reference to the Old Testament prophets.

Hebrews 6:1 refers to the laying of foundations. Just how

important such foundations are is illustrated by the fact that Jesus concluded his sermon with a parable which begins: "Every one then who hears these words of mine and does them will be like a wise man who built his house upon the rock . . .". Then he goes on to speak of the man who also hears his words, but does not do them, and describes him as a foolish man who builds his house upon the sand. Eventually, when both houses are subjected to the same tests of rain, flood and wind, the one built on the rock stands firm, whilst the one built on sand collapses—"and great was the fall of it" (Matthew 7:24–27).

The issue here is not faith, but obedience to the word of the Lord. Both men hear the word; the difference between them is that whilst one obeys, the other fails to do so. Initial faith is implied in both cases, but it is the works of faith which are the distinguishing mark in the case of the wise man.

This parable is clearly intended to emphasize the teaching which precedes it. Jesus wanted to establish first of all that what he had come to do and to teach was consistent with the moral teaching of the Law and the Prophets. What is brought before us in the Sermon is the foundational truth of the holiness of the Kingdom of God, and hence of the holiness which becomes those who will inherit the Kingdom. Without an understanding of those divine standards, how could men realize their fallenness and unfitness, and their need of a Saviour? As Paul says: "The law is our schoolmaster to bring us to Christ, that we might be justified by grace" (Galatians 3:24AV).

So it is not "justification by faith" which is in view here. Rather it is the quality of life which is necessary to inherit the Kingdom. This is the message of Hebrews throughout. It is "the great salvation" of Hebrews 2:3 which the writer warns the "holy brethren" that even they neglect at their peril. It is that aspect of "eternal salvation" (referred to in Hebrews 5:9) which is given by the Son "to all who obey him". These are the ones who are referred to later in our chapter (verse 12) as those "who through faith and patience inherit the promises".

In the parable in Matthew 7 there are two builders, one

The Exhortation (2)

building on rock, the other on sand. In Hebrews 6 the analogy is of those who keep laying the same foundation but fail to "go on" to build anything constructive on it. In both scriptures, the basic question is whether we are hearing the word of the Lord, and if so, whether we are obeying that word.

Further clarification of this "foundation" theme is provided by Paul in 1 Corinthians 3:9–17:

> For we are God's fellow-workers; you are God's field, God's building. According to the grace of God given to me, like a skilled master builder I laid a foundation, and another man is building upon it . . . . For no other foundation can any one lay than that which is laid, which is Jesus Christ. Now if any one builds on the foundation with gold, silver, precious stones, wood, hay, straw—each man's work will become manifest; for the Day will disclose it, because it will be revealed with fire, and the fire will test what sort of work each one has done. If the work which any man has built on the foundation survives, he will receive a reward. If any man's work is burned up, he will suffer loss, though he himself will be saved, but only as through fire. Do you not know that you are God's temple and that God's Spirit dwells in you? If any one destroys God's temple, God will destroy him. For God's temple is holy, and that temple you are.

Paul says here that he is a foundation layer—that is his special calling. Other men will build on foundations he has laid, and his concern is that they take care how they build on it.

Primarily, it seems, it is gifted leaders he has in mind. But as he develops his theme it is evident that the warning: "Let each man take care how he build upon it" reaches out to embrace all kinds of "work" which may be built on the one foundation, by any member of the Body of Christ.

Verse 11 should be particularly noted: "No other foundation can any one lay than that which is laid, which is Jesus Christ." If this statement appears to be at variance with the reference in Hebrews 6 where the foundation is of "repentance from dead works, etc . . ." this is explained by the different classes of people addressed. Both classes were Christians. But whereas the Hebrew brethren had a solid background of Old Testament teaching, the Corinthians were not so favoured. They had no such "schoolmaster" to bring them to Christ. On the contrary, for them, conversion to Christ meant a complete break with their pagan cultural background.

So in 1 Corinthians 3 Paul is speaking to people who, in terms of the Kingdom of God, had previously no valid spiritual foundations. Yet, as he shows them in this epistle, that in no way precludes them from participation in all the benefits made available under the terms of the New Covenant. "We preach Christ crucified, a stumbling block to Jews and folly to Gentiles, but to those who are called, both Jews and Greeks, Christ the power of God and the wisdom of God" (1 Cor 1:23,24).

Jesus Christ is their only foundation; and in terms of justification that is true for all New Covenant saints, Jews and Gentiles alike. Having no background knowledge of the law of God, everything these Corinthians were to learn as "those sanctified in Christ Jesus, called to be saints" stemmed from that foundational relationship which had been established when they first committed themselves to Christ, confessing him as their Saviour and Lord.

However, verse 12 also shows us that the fact that the Corinthians had lacked the privilege of a godly upbringing in their pre-Christian days did not exempt them from the responsibilities which the Lord placed on those privileged Jews to whom he spoke in the parable in Matthew 7. Whether a Christian is of Jewish or non-Jewish origin, at the judgment seat of Christ, "the fire will test what sort of work each one has done", and the rewards will be given accordingly.

So foundations are of supreme importance. And as we have seen, in the matter of the justification of the sinner the only valid foundation, as Paul declares, is Jesus Christ. But there is more to the building of a house than laying a good foundation.

My wife and I began our married life in rented rooms. One day a good Christian builder friend said to me: "David, if you can find a plot of land, I'll build you a house." We were then living in the "austerity" period after the 1939/44

The Exhortation (2)

war when, because of the shortage of materials, very few building permits were being issued by the authorities, and building plots were hard to come by.

However, we put an advert in the local paper and got one reply, offering us a plot in a pleasant area. There was something else about this plot which was particularly interesting. A foundation had already been laid on it for a small house, for which the owner told us planning approval had been obtained ten years or so before. It seems that after getting his plans approved he had become impatient to start building and decided to go ahead before he received the building permit. That had been about the time of the outbreak of the war, and he had never got beyond the laying of the foundation. There the plot remained all through the war and when we went to look at it the foundation was almost entirely hidden beneath grass and weeds.

Our builder friend quickly made an inspection of the plot, and came back with the report that the foundations were sound. We bought the plot, and put in an application for a building permit. It was late autumn, and—as we discovered—the local authorities had just received from the Ministry of Housing a further small, and quite unexpected, allocation of permits. So our application was granted, with one proviso: the building had to be commenced before the end of the year. "No problem", our friend assured us. The approved plans were passed over to him, and on the 31st December he drove a few pegs into the ground to establish that building had officially commenced.

Nine months later, when we moved into our new home, we invited our friends to come and have a look at it. What their comments were, I cannot remember. But there was one very important feature of the house which they never saw and about which probably they were not particularly interested—the foundations. Yet, when the plot first came into our possession, and in the weeks before the bricklayers and carpenters arrived, the importance of the foundations had been much impressed on our minds in connection with the home we hoped to have built on them. Our builder friend had a reputation second to none, and he put into our house the best possible materials available, and did a good job.

Foundations are important; equally so, what is built on them. We used to sing: "On Christ the solid rock I stand; all other ground is sinking sand." That's a wonderful testimony. But how truly alive are we to what Paul is saying, in this passage in 1 Corinthians, about taking care what we are building on that one foundation?

He declares emphatically: "the Day will disclose what sort of work each one has done." Again, in 2 Corinthians 5:10, he says: "For we must all appear before the judgment seat of Christ, so that each one may receive good or evil, according to what he has done in the body."

The fire will test what sort of work it is: whether of the durable quality of gold, silver, or precious stones—which is building "par excellence"—or of destructible materials such as wood, hay or straw. We know that in ourselves we do not have the resources to build, in spiritual terms, with gold, silver and precious stones. So how can we hope to acquire such materials, and the necessary building skills? The answer is that we do not build at our own charges, or according to our own specifications, or in dependence on any native skill we may have. Paul says in verse 9: "We are God's fellow-workers; you are God's field, God's building." In verse 16, he says, further: "Do you not know that you are God's temple and that God's Spirit dwells in you? If any one destroys God's temple, God will destroy him. God's temple is holy, and that temple you are."

"The Day will disclose (or declare) it." Then what? Verse 14 says plainly: "If the work which any man has built on the foundation survives, he will receive a reward. If any man's work is burned up, he will suffer loss, though he himself will be saved, but only as through fire."

It will be helpful if we look at these three "foundation" passages together and endeavour to discover how they support and reinforce each other on this important theme.

(1) In the parable which concludes the Sermon on the Mount, Jesus meets the Jews on their own ground of the Law and the Prophets, and warns them that outward conformity to the Law avails for nothing without an inner

response to its moral requirements. In the day of reckoning, those who "hear and do not" will be like the man who builds on sand. Their house will collapse; in other words, their work will be destroyed.

(2) In 1 Corinthians 3, Paul also meets the converted Corinthians on their own ground. He warns them that, though their feet are firmly planted on the solid rock, Jesus Christ, they must take care how they build thereon. How, and what, they build will determine what reward, if any, they receive in the Day of Christ. For what is built of destructible materials will be destroyed, though the builder himself will be saved, "but only as through fire".

(3) Coming back to Hebrews 6, we note that those addressed there are of the same nationality and religious background as those whom the Lord addressed in the Sermon on the Mount. But they are said to have been "enlightened". That is, they had come to personal faith in, and commitment to, Christ. So the one true foundation had been laid in their lives, just as it had been laid in the lives of the Corinthian Christians.

So far, so good. But what evidently concerned the writer is that they appeared to have settled back into a religious rut of "sound principles"—or what the writer calls "the elementary doctrine of Christ". There was nothing wrong with the principles, or the doctrine. What is wrong, however, is that, their excellent foundation nothwithstanding, they are no longer hearing the Lord. They are content simply to hold on to "the basics of the faith". They have lost any inclination to learn what the Lord has to teach them further concerning his purpose for them in relation to his Kingdom.

The lesson here for us today is very relevant; especially for those of us who reckon that we too have had a sound upbringing in biblical principles. It is not that we have to abandon our sound theological foundation (if indeed we have one) in order to move on into "kingdom living". Not a bit of it. The teaching of the New Testament is that true discipleship, which is based firmly on devotion to the Lord personally, will lead to devotion to his Word. "If you love me," says the Lord, "you will keep my commandments."

The message in each of these three passages is essentially the same. It is those who hear the word of the Lord and obey it to whom is promised fruitfulness and rewards in "the Day of the Lord". In Hebrews, as in Matthew and 1 Corinthians, the writer has a warning for the disobedient, though the analogies used vary. The warning which follows at verse 4 is very important, and later we shall devote a whole chapter to it. Our present discussion, however, requires that we look briefly at the analogy at verse 7 with which it concludes:

> For land which has drunk the rain that often falls upon it, and brings forth vegetation useful for those for whose sake it is cultivated, receives a blessing from God. But if it bears thorns and thistles, it is worthless and near to being cursed; its end is to be burned.

In 1 Corinthians, Paul introduces two classes of materials. Here, in Hebrews, the comparison is between two classes of land; ie: that which produces "useful vegetation", and that which produces "thorns and thistles". In 1 Corinthians, it is the destructible materials—wood, hay, straw—which are burnt up. Here, it is the land's worthless product of thorns and thistles which is consigned to the flames.

In neither case, is all lost. Concerning the man who built with shoddy materials, Paul makes a point of saying: "He himself will be saved; but only through fire". In Hebrews, the writer says of the land which produces only thorns and thistles, "It is near to being cursed." But it is not cursed. The significance of these scriptures was realized by an old man who had been converted near the end of a godless life. In reply to somebody who congratulated him on his salvation, he said: "My soul is saved; but my life has been lost." He had been "saved, yet so as through fire".

Each of these three scriptures emphasizes the foundational imperatives implicit in the Gospel of the Kingdom. Each urges on those who hear the word of the Kingdom their responsibility to obey that word. Jesus is the mediator of a New Covenant. These scriptures remind us of our accountability to him as covenantees, within the Covenant's terms.

Remembering Paul's statement: "You are God's field"; we

The Exhortation (2)

should ask ourselves: "Am I God's field? Has the Lord laid in me a good foundation? Has he begun a good work in me?" If we have any doubts as to how to answer these questions, the sooner we move on to the one foundation of Jesus Christ, the better. If we have already done that, then, as these scriptures clearly teach us, it is from that starting-point we are to move on in our calling as fellow-workers with Christ.

We are "God's field". In one of the Lord's parables, the Kingdom of God is likened to a man who found treasure in a field, and sold all he had to purchase it. In the same way, because God saw in us something of infinite worth, he purchased us at the price of the precious life-blood of his dear Son. Furthermore, he has drawn up plans and laid the foundation of what he desires to build on his purchased possession.

The scriptures we have been looking at, however, show that we are not simply materials held impassively in the Lord's hands. We are God's fellow-workers. This does not apply only to the apostolic ministry to which he refers as he introduces the passage, for he goes on to say: "Let each man take care how he builds." We are all to be builders; and although we do not build at our own expense or merely according to our own natural ability, we are held responsible as to how and what we build.

Following the passage in 1 Corinthians 3, we should notice that at verse 16 Paul enlarges on this reference to "God's building" (verse 9): "Do you not know that you are God's temple, and that God's Spirit dwells in you?" Though the analogy has changed, the message is the same.

In one sense, Paul is speaking here prophetically. "God's temple"—whether this is taken to signify the individual believer, or the Church as a whole, or a local church such as the one to which this letter was sent—is still in the process of being built. Yet, in God's plan, we are even now, individually and collectively, "God's temple", and that temple is "holy".

Such is the divine intention. Yet the warnings in this epistle, and in the New Testament as a whole, underline the fact that divine intention does not eliminate human responsibility. The question: "Do you not know that you are God's temple, and that God's Spirit dwells in you?" is not put simply to inform. Clearly it is a challenge, and a warning, as is shown by what follows: "If any one destroys God's temple, God will destroy him. For God's temple is holy, and that temple you are."

It is an essential feature of the Gospel of the Kingdom that privilege and responsibility go together; and the honour or abuse of privilege will both receive their due reward. In this connection, a passage in Hebrews 3:4–6 should be noted:

> (For every house is built by some one, but the builder of all things is God.) Now Moses was faithful in all God's house as a servant, to testify to the things which were to be spoken later, but Christ was faithful over God's house as a son. And we are his house if we hold fast our confidence and pride in our hope firm to the end.

"We are his house IF . . .". Once again we are confronted by that conditional "if", linking the divine intention with our human responsibility. We are to hold fast our confidence—not in ourselves, but in the one who is said to have been "faithful over God's house as a son". And we are to "hold fast . . . our pride in our hope"; that is, our hope of the inheritance. This is the "blessed hope" to which reference will again be made at the end of this passage in Hebrews 6. "Hold it fast!" says this writer, ". . . firm to the end".

"Let us go on," he exhorts. On, that is, in partnership with the Lord in the great work of the building of his house; on "to maturity", as we walk with him and are instructed by him in the mysteries of the Kingdom of God.

"And this we will do, if God permits." Once again, we note the conditional "if". "If God permits."

The man from whom I bought the plot was prevented from building on it because he didn't have a permit. Was it because these Hebrew Christians had no permit that they had made no progress beyond laying the foundations? Is that why so many Christians have never made headway in their Christian lives since the foundations of faith were laid in them—in some cases—many years ago? No building permit? Have they put in their application at the throne of grace and had it returned, rubber-stamped "not granted"?

Nothing in the Hebrew epistle, or elsewhere in the New Testament, gives credence to any such claim. On the contrary, the message throughout is that not only is a permit to build in the house of the Lord the birthright of every born-again child of God, but also that it is our responsibility to claim it. We are the Lord's purchased possession; we are temples of the Holy Spirit; we are "the called ones ... according to his purpose".

It is, indeed, for our encouragement that the writer rounds off his exhortation at this point with "if God permits", reminding us that, from start to finish in this great enterprise, we are completely dependent on the grace of God.

That is good news! We do not have to move an inch in dependence on our own resources. "By the grace of God I am what I am," says Paul. The Lord has not handed us a plan and a programme and a time-schedule, and told us to get on with it. He has personally come on to the site to supervise the job, and to be personally involved in it. We are fellow-workers with him. That's what makes it all so worthwhile, so purposeful, and ultimately, so rewarding, to "go on".

How tragic to be one of God's children with access to all the resources of his grace, and with that privileged permit in your possession, and yet to end up with nothing except a tumbledown wooden shack which in the Day of the Lord will be burnt to ashes!

It need not be. Let us take encouragement from the prayer with which this great treatise on the high priestly work of the Lord Jesus is brought to its conclusion (Hebrews 13:20):

> Now may the God of peace who brought again from the dead our Lord Jesus, the great shepherd of the sheep, by the blood of the eternal covenant, equip you with everything good that you may do his will, working in you that which is pleasing in his sight, through Jesus Christ; to whom be glory for ever and ever. Amen.

Chapter Four

The Exhortation (3)

IN THE EXHORTATION PASSAGE IN HEBREWS 5 THE WRITER identifies three symptoms of the spiritual condition of the Christians to whom he is writing.

Firstly, they had become "dull of hearing"; inattentive, that is, to the word of the Lord. Then, as a consequence, they had remained unskilled in that word and spiritually immature.

A further serious consequence is implied in the general statement with which the writer sums up the passage in verse 14. He says: "Solid food is for the mature, for those who have their faculties trained by practice to distinguish good from evil." In other words, behind the more obvious symptoms of inattention and immaturity lay the less obvious —but serious—disability of lack of spiritual discernment.

From the immediate context of this passage, and of the epistle as a whole, we see that the spiritual state of these brethren is of great concern to the writer. Yet, though he is concerned, he is by no means despairing. For, in spite of the force of the personal exhortations and warnings with which the main theme of the epistle is frequently interspersed, Hebrews is essentially an epistle of hope—what the writer calls "the better hope" of the New Covenant. Throughout the epistle, the promise of the inheritance and the warning of possible forfeiture through disobedience, are constantly held in tension. But always the bias is on the positive side, as when, following the warning in chapter 6, the writer says: "Though we speak thus, yet in your case, beloved, we feel sure of better things that belong to salvation."

So we cannot claim the promises, and disclaim the warnings. To do so is to play into the hands of the enemy. Hebrews is a much-quoted book, but if we only hear its promises and refuse to heed its warnings and exhortations, then we are simply not hearing the Lord in his Word at all.

The Exhortation (3)

This was what concerned the writer. These brethren had not departed from the faith, though he does not fail to warn them of that possibility. They were still sound in the faith in the sense that they stood firmly on the foundation of "the elementary doctrine of Christ". But they were no longer hearing the Lord. Does that sound like a fair description of many Christians living near the end of the twentieth century? Though our cultural and religious backgrounds may differ from that of those first century Christians, the truth is that this epistle is as relevant for us today as it was for them. That is why we must come back to this passage in Hebrews 5 to consider its practical implications in relation to influences and pressures to which we are subjected today.

The statement "Solid food is for the mature, for those who have their faculties trained to distinguish good from evil", embodies an important spiritual principle. Throughout the New Testament, beginning with the teaching of the Lord, we are warned to be constantly on our guard against Satan, who under many different guises—and especially masquerading as an angel of light—is ceaselessly endeavouring to deceive the people of God. Particularly is this to be expected at the end of the age when, it is predicted, many will depart from the faith by giving heed to deceitful spirits and doctrines of demons (1 Timothy 4:1).

Whether we are living now in the last of "the last days" or not, it is certain we are nearer that time than ever before. Nor do we need to be experts in prophecy to realize that a fierce conflict is already raging in "the heavenly places". Yet how many of us are truly alive to this situation, or take it seriously? At a time when, more than ever, we should be wide awake to "the signs of the times" as reflected in current trends in world affairs, these three symptoms of inattentiveness to God's word, spiritual immaturity, and lack of spiritual discernment are rife, even among many who are recognized as leaders among the people of God.

"Hearing the Lord", means hearing "the whole counsel of God"—the warnings as well as the promises. The Lord has indeed given us many wonderful promises—and, incidentally, that word "promise" occurs more times in Hebrews than in any other New Testament book—but we cannot afford to ignore the contexts in which these promises are found.

In chapter 4:1, there is a promise of entering "(God's) rest". That is a wonderful prospect! But the whole verse reads: "Therefore, while the promise of entering his rest remains, let us fear lest any of you be judged to have failed to reach it." When we come to chapter 6, we read (verse 13) that "God made a promise to Abraham," and (verse 15) "Abraham, having endured patiently, obtained the promise."

But Abraham was an Old Testament character—so what has all that to do with us? The answer is that Abraham is introduced here, as elsewhere in the New Testament, as an example to those of us who, under the terms of the New Covenant, are "the heirs of the promise" (verse 17). Going back to verse 12, we read: "so that you may not be sluggish, but imitators of those who through faith and patience inherit the promises". Note, it is not through faith alone that the inheritance is gained. It is "through faith and *patience*".

In similar vein Paul, in that triumphant eighth chapter of Romans (where he speaks of being "more than conquerors through him that loved us"), says: "We are children of God, and if children, then heirs, heirs of God and fellow heirs with Christ, *provided we suffer with him* in order that we may be glorified with him."

This conditional element is an integral part of the Gospel of the Kingdom.

Nobody knows this better than Satan. He knows, moreover, that Christ's declared objectives are in direct opposition to his own avowed ambition to make himself like the Most High, and to set his throne on high (Isaiah 14). That is why he does all he can to hinder the proclamation of the Gospel of the Kingdom, and is very happy when "cheap grace" is proclaimed as the totality of the gospel, and "the word of the kingdom" is made of little or no effect, by dilution, distortion, or even by plain denial.

We know that Satan is the prince of the power of the air, the spirit who is now at work in the sons of disobedience. But let us not suppose that we who claim to have our feet firmly planted on "redemption ground" therefore carry some kind of personal immunity from his attacks. At the end of his first epistle, John recognizes two distinct categories of people when he says: "We know we are of God, and the whole world is in the power of the evil one." Yet he also makes it clear in his epistles and elsewhere, that Satan does not observe the ground rules and stick to his side of the boundary. That is why we must hear God if we are to have our faculties trained to distinguish good from evil.

There was never a time when this was more necessary than now. In the secular press there are frequent reports of cultist activity, not only outside what are called "the historic churches", but increasingly within them also. Much of this is exceedingly insidious. When trusted and gifted church leaders become involved (sometimes quite unconsciously, one suspects) in attractive teachings, the original source of which must be said to be highly questionable, the need for scripture-based discernment becomes even more evident.

Further into the cult scene there is the vast range of material on many booksellers' and newsagents' shelves, plugging demonism, witchcraft, spiritism and the like. Much of this has, more recently, come under the aegis of the emerging and ubiquitous New Age movement, which is unquestionably satanic, and is aimed at all levels of intelligence from academics to young children.

We might ask, how comes it that so many of those who fall into the hands of these false teachers are, or were at one time, connected to churches within what is commonly known as "the historic stream"? Would that not have meant that they heard the Bible read, and were familiar with many of the grand old hymns which are rich in Christian teaching? All that may be true. But in how many churches is the Bible read other than in small prescribed doses as part of a liturgical routine, or as the starting-point for a ten-minute sermon? How much serious Bible-teaching is given in the majority of churches, even among Evangelicals? How many church leaders are genuine Bible-believers?

There are, of course, many exceptions to this general pattern of contemporary church life. But, by and large, the situation is such that it is hardly surprising that the majority of church-going people are spiritually starved. Is it any wonder, therefore, that when the enthusiastic cult missionary arrives on their door-step bringing a message of life and hope, they are disposed to listen awhile, just in case there might be something in it for them? Not every fish rises to the bait. But these dedicated missionaries do not toil for nothing. In Britain today it is estimated that there are approximately one hundred different cults; many of them claiming to be "Christian". Between them, over the last few years, they have caught thousands of gullible, uninstructed seekers after truth, most of whom are people who formerly attended some denominational church (and some continue to do so). Lacking adequate knowledge of the basics of the Christian faith, these converts have been unable to detect the poison in the attractive religious package offered them, and they have swallowed the lot.

They may not, of course, have been true Christians in the first instance. Be that as it may, it is evident that previously they had been unsatisfied and spiritually insecure, and when the cult religion was presented to them, it seemed to offer them what they needed. And now they are "hooked" into a religious system which belongs to the apostle John's "other" category which lies "in the power of the evil one".

By contrast, some of us may claim (again quoting John) that "we know we are of God". We are "born again"; we say our prayers and read our Bibles; we are committed members of some "live" church or fellowship. Within our chosen Christian framework—denominational, evangelical, catholic, charismatic, restorationist, however we like to define it— we feel secure, even satisfied. When the cult evangelist comes to the door, we say—politely—"Not today, thank you"—and send him (or her) on his (or her) way.

If, on the other hand, we do decide to invite these people in, we may find it a very challenging experience. Many of them are quite new converts to their faith. Yet they boldly come to our door, and within the guidelines of their teaching often acquit themselves with considerable competence, much more impressively than do many of our supposedly

The Exhortation (3)

well-grounded "born again" Christians when challenged as to their faith. There are, of course, many exceptions. But it is a sobering thought that whilst cult converts are generally strongly motivated to study their text-books, and actively witness for their cause, most Christians remain comparatively untaught in God's word, and many seem reluctant to testify. What is the reason for this?

Our passage in Hebrews has the answer. The writer recognizes that these Hebrew Christians had a good foundation, being well-versed in the elementary doctrine of Christ. As such, therefore, they provide a good prototype of the soundly-based Christian. Yet it is to them that his exhortations and warnings are addressed because they had become dull of hearing and consequently remain spiritually immature and lacking in spiritual discernment.

We might be interested to know what were the special circumstances which had provoked this state of affairs. But it is more to the point for us—if we agree that these symptoms are true for us today—to enquire why this should be so, and what is needed to remedy the condition. Perhaps an illustration based on a not untypical contemporary domestic scene might help us in our enquiry.

Jack and Jane Brown are a church-going Christian couple. They have settled down for an evening's relaxation after a busy day. The children are in bed. The front door bell rings. Jack answers to a couple of cheerful young men. They ask Jack if he is interested in the state of the world and what the future holds for us all. Jack decides to play it safe. In answer to his enquiry, the callers confirm they are Jehovah's Witnesses. So Jack politely tells them he does not wish to discuss their views at present, and bids them "Good-day". Returning to the lounge, he and Jane devote their attention to an honoured permanent guest who occupies the focal point in the room. His name is Johnnie TV.

Johnnie is no mere caller. He is not even a paying guest. Carefully chosen by the Browns from a number of competitors he is actually paid for the privilege of occupying the place of honour in their lounge. Why? Because of his ability to provide for their entertainment an extensive repertoire of "doctored" news, spectator sport, loaded documentaries, music, drama, and—in what is known as "the God slot"—religion.

It is a mixed bag, and—along with the trivia and the trash—there are some very good things too. But frankly, it is astonishing to discover to what programmes many Christians allow themselves and their families to be exposed. Occasionally, concern is expressed about the corrupting material appearing on the screen, even in programmes dubiously classified as "family viewing". Sadly, however, many seem to have capitulated to this colossal insult to human dignity as though it were an inescapable fact of life.

"TV has come to stay", it used to be said: as though that were the last word on the subject. This could be said also of video recorders, and cable television; and doubtless there are other electronic delights in the pipeline to fill the ever-increasing hours of leisure we are promised in the future. "So we just gotta get wired up buddy, and take what comes"—is that the only way we can handle this issue?

Let us look at some relevant facts. (1) If Johnny TV comes to stay in my home, it is by my invitation, and at my expense. (2) If he comes in, then assuming I'm the head of the house, how this expensive and talkative guest behaves is my responsibility. (3) That responsibility continues without intermission; it does not cease when I am away from the home. So, if I have children left at home on their own, or in charge of a vulnerable and immature baby-sitter, I am responsible for everything they see on TV during my absence. (4) I have a right to shut up, smash up, or dismiss this guest at any time.

It is as simple as that. What goes for TV, goes also for video, radio, and all the rest of the media fraternity, should any of them come into my home and threaten its sanctity as a "house of God".

After all, we are not yet living in a country ruled by some Big Brother system which sends around a surveillance squad to ensure that our two-way TV is in good working order, and we are dutifully attending to all the prescribed programmes. My home may not be a castle, but, by God's

The Exhortation (3)

grace, it can and should be a sanctuary; a dwelling place for God. The only "Big Brother" entitled to boss my Christian home—and that of every true Christian—is Jesus, the Son of God.

Before we leave the media scene, there is another specialized field to which we should give attention; one which is of particular interest to the younger generation, and therefore highly significant in relation to the church of the future. I refer to what is known as "pop" or "rock" music.

Before I am challenged as to my qualifications for expressing any views on this theme, let me explain that I am drawing exclusively on the writing of an expert, Alasdair Black. In a small book entitled: "The New Babylon", he says: "Every Thursday night . . . the television is switched on, the channel has been chosen, the clock strikes 7.30; and from within the set comes a voice welcoming you to 'Top of the Pops' . . . there then proceeds forty minutes of the latest news and sounds from the religious world of music."

This writer can hardly be said to have been an old fuddy-duddy. On the book's cover it is stated that (at the time of writing) he was eighteen years old, so he ought to have known what he was talking about. This is what he says: "Music has become the new universal religion of the young . . . As in all good religions, there are several different denominations, with a new branch forming every few months." At the time of writing (which, it must be said, was some time ago), "the major denominations (were) the progressive church of Heavy Metal, the church of the Mods (whose congregations have been dwindling), the 'anti-religious' church of Punk, the advanced new Romantics, and the reformed church of Rock-a-Billy."

Once you have selected your particular "church" it appears that your life is shaped accordingly. Hairstyle and dress conform to the approved stereotype. Services of communal worship are attended at discos and concerts. Private devotions are regularly attended at the family altar of Hi-Fi or Radio 1. And the highlight of the year, if you can afford it (which you probably can), will be attendance at a 'religious' festival of music. These festivals tend to be strictly "denominational", and are supported by thousands of pilgrims, most of whom belong to that particular "denomination". "Concerts are the churches of today," says one of their noted celebrants. Many who are involved in this scene are unashamedly idolatrous. Pop, or rock, culture is a religion which offers its devotees a form of escape from the intolerable boredom of materialism; an attempt to plug the God-shaped blank in lives devoid of purpose.

Alasdair says that whereas in the past the bands were advocating the three basic reliefs of sex, drugs, and "music", what has now emerged, in addition, is the advocacy of supernatural-occult experiences as the answer to life's void. There is no doubt that Satan's purpose is to capture this generation for explicit, overt commitment to his cause; and in recent years he has made considerable progress towards achieving his objective. Some groups are known to be thoroughly immersed in Satanism. Star performers have declared their hatred of God and their support of the cause of Satan. Others appear to be mere dupes of Satan who are not too sure or happy about what's happening to them. One of them is quoted as saying: "I don't know if I am a medium of some outside force; frankly I hope it is not what I think: Satan."

Alasdair makes special mention of a young female singer who was voted No 1 singer in the British rock and pop awards some time ago. She says: "There is a psychic war going on out there between good and evil", and it may well be the case that she does not realize on which side she is fighting. One of her numbers is a track about the supposed defeat of Christ by Satan. Such numbers have been broadcasted at peak viewing times, and are heard by young fans who are hardly into their teens.

Do *Christians* realize that this "psychic war" is going on "out there", as this young performer says? Are *our* spiritual faculties trained so that we can recognize the spiritual source of what is being fed into impressionable minds (including our own) through this or any other medium? If so, how are we handling the issue as it affects our own lives, and the lives of our children, and others within the sphere of our responsibility? Do we simply shrug our shoulders and say: "It's pretty awful; but what can we do about it? Let's

The Exhortation (3)

hope they will eventually grow out of it." Or do we mumble something about "the generation gap"?

Let us remember we are not talking about mere kids' stuff. There is plenty of that; some of it quite good, some distinctly bad, and some fairly indifferent. We are looking at concoctions which are poisonous, and ought to be labelled as such.

I hasten to add, however, that there is nothing intrinsically wrong with these modern methods of communication any more than there is with the more ancient ones of letter writing, or the "bush telegraph". It is the use to which they are put which is the issue. On the positive side, we can be thankful for every good use to which the media is being put in these days, including the spread of the good news of the gospel, not only through secular channels, but through Christian ones too.

For too long however, Christians have disregarded the biblical categories of light and darkness; of truth and error; of good and evil. We are not talking about a mere "generation gap", but about the gulf which separates the children of light from the children of darkness.

> What fellowship has light with darkness?
> What accord has Christ with Belial?
> Or what has a believer in common with an unbeliever?
> What agreement has the temple of God with idols?
> For we are the temple of the living God . . .
> Therefore come out from them, and be separate from them,
>   says the Lord, and touch nothing unclean;
> then I will welcome you, and I will be a father to you,
> and you shall be my sons and daughters, says the Lord Almighty.

Let the challenge of those words of Paul from 2 Corinthians 6 sink into out hearts.

This is *not* to lay down rules as to what other people shall, or shall not, have in their homes. In the long run, such rules can be counter-productive. Like drugs, they act from outside our own volition, and hence weaken our God-given ability to seek his guidance in determining his will for us personally in the conduct of our lives and homes.

The writer to the Hebrews did not do this. Rather, he

urged the brethren to hear God for themselves and to move on with God, in accordance with the marvellously attractive terms of the New Covenant.

No longer were they to conform to a code of laws written on tablets of stone. But that did not mean that they had become law-less. The time had come for the fulfilment of the Lord's promise through Jeremiah (31:33,34):

> I will put my law within them, and I will write it upon their hearts . . . no longer shall each man teach his neighbour and each his brother saying, "Know the LORD," for they shall all know me, from the least of them to the greatest, says the LORD.

Knowing the Lord personally; receiving his word into our hearts; this is basic New Covenant spirituality. The men and women whom the Lord calls to serve him in the cause of the Kingdom are not mere conformists to a stereotyped pattern, driven on from behind like a herd of sheep. They are those who hear the voice of the Shepherd and follow him of their own volition. They are impelled by an inner urge to seek out and find the way he has chosen for them. That is their choice. It is in the company of the Shepherd that they become increasingly aware of the activities of the unholy trinity of the thief, the wolf, and the hireling, and they know how to deal with them now. For since they have learned to heed the Shepherd's voice, their faculties have been trained to distinguish good from evil.

Hearing the voice of the Lord—that, basically, is the answer to our problem, and it is for this reason primarily that we must resist those alien influences which threaten to sabotage that basic requirement. This is the very antithesis of legalism. We have been liberated from sin's bondage and have been called into the fellowship of God's Son.

That is true liberty, for whom the Son sets free, is free indeed. So it is from the privileged position of "sonship" that we face up to the challenges which confront us at the end of this twentieth century.

I have focused attention on the media because this happens to be one of the most powerful influences for evil

The Exhortation (3)

in our society today. Even secular humanists acknowledge this. But of course the enemy has plenty of other channels through which to pursue his relentless vendetta against the Church of Christ. I may hate everything electronic, and go to live on some remote island somewhere, but Satan will still find ways of diverting my attention away from the Lord. So it is for each of us to discover for ourselves what particularly threatens to destroy *our* capacity to hear the Shepherd's voice.

All the same, we should face up to the fact that the media has become one of our major challenges. To treat this challenge as though it did not exist, or is of no great significance; or to dodge it because it is too hot to handle, is the height of irresponsibility.

How dare we tolerate the infiltration of moral pollution into our homes—through whatever channel it comes—simply because it takes discipline and moral courage to tackle it? What sort of parents or church leaders are we, if we allow ourselves to be pushed around by the accepted norms and mores of a generation which is heading for holocaust? What our Christian friends think is right for themselves and their families is their responsibility. Ours, if we claim to be the Lord's committed disciples, is to seek him personally to find out what he requires *us* to do.

When the Philistines invaded Israel, it was not king Saul who rose to the challenge of their champion Goliath, but a young shepherd lad named David. Out in the wilderness, caring for his father's sheep, David had learned to listen to God, and how to use a sling. He had been trained by experience to distinguish good from evil. What is more, he had learned to love the good and hate the evil; to love the ways of God and to hate the ways of wickedness. Here was a young man who had in his bones the fire of a living faith in the Lord of hosts; and, in his heart, the unquenchable ambition that "all the earth may know that there is a God in Israel".

That was the measure of David's spiritual maturity; not the number of years he had lived. It was not personal ambition which spurred him on—not self-glory—but a whole-hearted commitment to the glory of Jehovah, the

God of Israel. Nor did he take up Goliath's challenge presumptuously; "I come to you in the name of the Lord of hosts, the God of the armies of Israel, whom you have defied"—that was his approach. And within minutes he had Goliath under his feet. In the hour of Israel's crisis, it was the young man who had walked with God and listened to God, not proud Saul, who stood head and shoulders above his fellows; nor any of David's seven older brothers, who had emerged as the nation's deliverer.

Effective leadership, at whatever level of responsibility, whether in the home or in the church, starts with hearing the Lord, and his word. Early in his ministry, when Jesus wanted men to help him in his work, Mark tells us that he "called to him those whom he desired; and they came to him. And he appointed twelve to be with him."

These particular men, we know, were called to a special ministry. But is that not true of all the members of the Body of Christ? We are a "called" people. Earlier in Hebrews the writer addresses his readers (in chapter 3) as "holy brethren, who share in a heavenly call". When Paul wrote to the church at Corinth, it was to the whole church that he said: "Consider your call, brethren; not many of you were wise according to worldly standards, not many were powerful, not many were of noble birth; etc . . ." . But, their unimpressive record nothwithstanding, they were a "called" people. It simply underlines the fact that God's ways and standards are different from man's.

A good listener makes a good learner; and a good learner is the material out of which a good leader is made. I sometimes hear of young Christian men being referred to as "good leadership material". What we need to realize is that there is much more to spiritual leadership than, for example, a degree in sociology, or even a diploma in theology, or any other natural attainments and abilities. The first and most important step in our "call" is, like that of the Twelve, a call to be "with the Lord"; for it is only as we spend time in his company that we really "hear" him.

This needs to be realized by all who believe they have received a call from the Lord to serve him, whatever that call may involve. When Paul, in his second letter to the

Corinthians, wrote about his own call to the ministry of the Lord, this is what he said:

> Not that we are competent of ourselves to claim anything as coming from us; our competence is from God, who has made us competent to be ministers of a new covenant, not in a written code but in the Spirit; for the written code kills, but the Spirit gives life. (2 Corinthians 3:5,6)

Our enemy Satan is greater than Goliath; but the Lord whom we serve is greater than Satan. If there is a crisis of leadership today, as is often asserted, it is not because there are not enough men and women available with adequate intelligence and education and charisma. The shortage is of those who not only possess these basic natural qualities, but who are also "hearing" the Lord.

The reason why these Hebrew Christians remained immature, and lacked spiritual discernment, was not that they lacked intelligence or had no "foundations". It was because they had become "dull of hearing".

CHAPTER FIVE

Background to the Warning of Apostasy (Hebrews 6:4–8)

WHEN AT THIS POINT THE WRITER INVITES THE READER TO "leave the elementary doctrine of Christ, and go on to maturity", it might be assumed that this was a signal of his intention to return now to his main theme.

Instead, however, he now plunges into a solemn warning about the danger of apostasy. There is nothing in the immediate context to explain this, and we must look into the wider context of the epistle as a whole to find an explanation. Also, more importantly, it is there that we may find a key to the understanding of this admittedly difficult passage.

The main emphasis in Hebrews, as we have seen, is on the high priestly ministry of Jesus. But that ministry is not an end in itself. Behind that emphasis is the revelation of the Lord Jesus as the enthroned King in glory, and the divine purpose to bring many sons to glory in company with him.

Although these Hebrew Christians had grasped "the elementary doctrine of Christ" in so far as it provided them with assurance of deliverance from eternal judgment, whatever they may have been taught earlier about the hope of the inheritance—or "sonship"—seems to have been either forgotten or overlooked. This was particularly regrettable since their Old Covenant teaching should have prepared them for the further revelation now available to them. For the law, as this writer points out, had been "a shadow of good things to come" under the terms of a "new" and "better" covenant.

They knew that God's purpose in bringing his redeemed people out of Egypt had been that, under Moses's leadership, they should be brought into their inheritance in the land of Canaan. They knew that that generation failed to

Background to the Warning of Apostasy

enter into their inheritance because of rebellion and unbelief, and that similarly, later generations also came under divine judgment. Yet they had failed to grasp the spiritual implications for them of these historic events. As under the Old Covenant, so now under the New, the fulfilment of the divine purpose necessarily involved potential "sons" in a continuing discipline. In spite of their greater privileges, our writer fears that these brethren are in danger of treading the same downward path as their forefathers had trodden. Hence the main theme of this epistle is interspersed with warnings based, directly or by implication, on the sad story of the decline and fall of God's covenant people of that earlier age.

The first of these warnings follows a discussion in which the writer quotes seven Old Testament scriptures in support of a statement as to the superiority of the Son over angels. In his summing-up, he takes the argument even further when he says: "Are they not all ministering spirits sent forth to serve, for the sake of those who are to obtain (literally: 'be heirs of') salvation?"

To the orthodox Hebrew it would have been inconceivable that, under God, there could be any order of beings higher than angels. Was the writer then suggesting that there could be an order of manhood which would be elevated above angels, and served by them? That is precisely what he is asserting. This claim will be developed as he proceeds, and is implied in the warning which immediately follows:

> Therefore we must pay the closer attention to what we have heard, lest we drift away from it. For if the message declared by angels was valid and every transgression or disobedience received a just retribution, how shall we escape if we neglect such a great salvation?

As he proceeds, the writer is careful to identify this "great salvation":

> It was declared at first by the Lord, and it was attested to us by those who heard him, while God also bore witness by signs and wonders and various miracles and by gifts of the Holy Spirit distributed according to his own will.

He is saying, in effect, that the exalted nature of the One

who declared the message, and of the message itself, together with its divine authentication by signs and wonders and miracles, puts the hearers in a position of great responsibility to give the closest attention to what they have heard. For it is "we"—that is, the writer, and those to whom he writes—and, indeed, all God's New Covenant people—whom the angels are sent forth to serve; it is "we", in fact, who are the "heirs" of "such a great salvation".

This burden of the first warning will be re-echoed again and again later in the epistle. For example, in the concluding sentences of his "teaching" (12:25ff) the writer says:

> See that you do not refuse him who is speaking. For if they did not escape when they refused him who warned them on earth, much less shall we escape if we reject him who warns from heaven.

We should note how, in the Hebrews 2 reference, the writer identifies the "great salvation" as being the substance of a message which was "at first declared by the Lord". Therefore it is to the gospels that we must turn to find what the Lord taught, and what he instructed his disciples to teach. There we are introduced to a "salvation" message which the Lord himself referred to as "the Gospel of the Kingdom".

This incorporates two main features: (1) First, there is the foundational truth of God in Christ meeting the sinner's personal need of redemption, as summed up in that well-known verse, John 3:16. (2) The second, and actually, more prominent, feature is the invitation to enter, and become involved in, "the kingdom of our Lord and of his Christ" (Revelation 11:15).

This is constantly in view, not only in the teaching of Jesus, but also of his forerunner John the Baptist; and later, as we should expect, of Jesus's disciples. Both features are inseparable ingredients of the gospel which the Lord told his disciples was to be "preached throughout the whole world as a testimony to all nations" (Matthew 24:14). It ought not to be necessary to say that any programme of New Covenant teaching which does not incorporate both features is incomplete and misleading.

Background to the Warning of Apostasy 51

Pursuing his theme, the writer goes on to say (2:5): "For it was not to angels that God subjected the world to come, of which we are speaking." This leaves us in no doubt that he wants to focus his reader's attention on "the world to come", and that, in that "world" (or age), contrary to what might have been assumed, it is not angels to whom the responsibility of ruling is to be committed.

To whom then? We recall how the writer had previously drawn attention to the Son's superiority over the angels. It might have been expected therefore that, at this point, he would have stated unequivocally that that future commitment will be to the Son. But he does not actually say this. His more immediate reference had been to "the heirs of salvation". He still has these in view as, once again, he turns to the Psalms. "It has been testified somewhere" (Psalm 8),

> What is man that thou art mindful of him,
>   or the son of man, that thou carest for him?
> Thou didst make him for a little while lower
>   than the angels,
> thou hast crowned him with glory and honour,
>   putting everything in subjection under his feet.

So it is man—but man in a new exalted setting—man elevated above the angels, who is to be crowned with glory and honour, everything being put in subjection under his feet!

But can these lines from an Old Testament psalm still be regarded as prophecy which has yet to be fulfilled? Does not man's appalling record of disobedience to God's laws rule out any possibility of his still being chosen for a position of authority in the coming age? The writer is not unaware of the seeming incongruity of his claim. Yet he holds firmly to it, as he draws together the two parallel insights he had previously been developing.

He had spoken of the Son's superiority over angels, and of angels being ministering spirits to "heirs of salvation". This had been followed by the reference in Psalm 8 to man's exaltation to a position of glory and honour. Now he will show how both these insights are to be fulfilled in one great apocalyptic sequence arising out of an event which had taken place probably within the lifetime of most of his readers. Although the psalmist speaks of man being "crowned with glory and honour", with everything having been put under his feet, "we do not yet see everything in subjection to him", admits the writer:

> But we see Jesus, who for a little while was made lower than the angels, crowned with glory and honour because of the suffering of death, so that by the grace of God he might taste death for every one.

It is here that the human name of Jesus is first introduced in the epistle; and this, unmistakably, to emphasize the essential humanity of the person upon whom attention is now focused.

In the fulness of time, a man had appeared on earth who fulfilled all that the Father looks for in manhood. In Jesus, the Son of God has shared in flesh and blood; has partaken of human nature; has tasted death. And more. Because of the perfection of his human life, and of what he has accomplished, he is now crowned with glory and honour.

It is in this connection that the writer now refers specifically to the high priestly ministry of Jesus: "Therefore he had to be made like his brethren in every respect, so that he might become a merciful and faithful high priest in the service of God" (2:17). Two main features of that priestly ministry are then mentioned: (1) to make atonement for sins; (2) to strengthen his brethren so that they might be able to overcome temptation.

It is clear from the context of this passage that this priestly ministry did not merely provide "safety, certainty, and enjoyment" for New Covenant saints. It was related to the Father's "kingdom" plans. The bringing of many sons to glory is a superhuman task. They need not only a leader to direct them, but a high priest to plead for them when they err, and to renew and encourage them when they stumble or grow faint by the way. All this is with a view to the attainment of the "great salvation" to which they are heirs, but of which they are not, as yet, in possession.

Such an unfolding of the divine purpose, and of the divine

Background to the Warning of Apostasy

provision for the heirs of salvation, brings the writer to his first direct approach to the people to whom he is writing (3:1): "Therefore, holy brethren, who share in a heavenly call, consider Jesus, the apostle and high priest of our confession."

They are "holy brethren"; they share in "a heavenly call"; they have Jesus as their apostle and high priest. What a uniquely privileged company they are! This fact is established before anything else is said about them. In all that he reveals concerning the Father's plans, together with all the warnings and exhortations he addresses to these friends of his, the writer has always in mind the fact that, by divine favour, they are "holy brethren, who share in a heavenly call".

His reference to Jesus as "the apostle and high priest of our confession" would inevitably turn the thoughts of these Hebrew Christians to Moses, their great ancestral leader. This undoubtedly was the writer's intention, for Moses is introduced here at the starting-point of a new stage in the development of his theme. Jesus, our apostle and high priest, was faithful to him who appointed him, just as Moses was faithful in God's house. But Jesus is counted worthy of more glory than Moses as the builder of a house has more honour than a member of the household. Moses was faithful in God's house as a servant; but Christ was faithful over God's house as a son.

Such is the gist of what this writer is saying (3:2–6); and the introduction of the analogy of "God's house" (or household) provides a valuable, and significant, link between his "kingdom" vision and that of Paul and Peter in both of whose epistles the theme of "the household of God" is developed. For our present purpose, we need only to note the words in verse 6 with which this introductory passage concludes: "Christ was faithful over God's house as a son. And we are his house, if *we hold fast our conscience and pride in our hope, firm to the end.*"

In his first brief warning (2:3,4) the writer had warned his friends of the danger of drifting away from, or neglecting, "the great salvation". Evidently, that fearful possibility is still much in his mind. God's house (or household) is the sphere of his authority—that is—his "kingdom". Involvement in God's "household"—or "kingdom", then, is the ultimate goal of the heavenly call.

The writer's concern that his brethren shall not fail to reach that goal now brings him to his second warning, which provides the key to the understanding of all the subsequent warnings in this epistle.

He begins (3:7): "Therefore, as the Holy Spirit says . . .", followed by a quotation from Psalm 95. In that psalm King David makes an impassioned appeal to the people of Israel who were evidently in danger of turning away from the Lord. David reminds them of God's dealings with their forefathers four hundred years before, when they had rebelled against him at Kadesh-Barnea on their journey to the Promised Land. That incident is recorded in detail in Numbers 14. It is significant however that our writer chooses to look at it in the light of David's comments, rather than go back to the original account in Numbers. Taking the warning as given by David four hundred years after the original event, he updates it by a further six hundred years and applies it to these first century New Covenant saints.

By his reference to the words spoken by the Holy Spirit, he is clearly asserting that what he is now saying is not based on personal judgment. This application of an Old Testament warning to New Testament saints is given under the authority of the Holy Spirit; an assertion which, incidentally, underlines the unchanging character of God's dealings, in all ages, with his covenant people when they rebel against him.

Almost two thousand years have passed since Hebrews was written. But are not those of us who, by God's grace, claim to be disciples of Christ today, in the same relationship to God as were those first century believers? If so, then all that is set out in this passage is evidently as applicable to us in our "today" as it was to those to whom this epistle was originally sent. "Today" is, in fact, a key word in this warning passage, where it occurs five times. Three times the writer repeats the appeal: "Today, if you will hear his voice, do not harden your hearts, as in the rebellion . . ." It reminds us of his opening statement (1:1,2): "In these last

Background to the Warning of Apostasy

days God has spoken to us by [his] Son" and of the exhortation (2:1): "Therefore we must pay the closer attention to what we have heard, lest we drift away from it." "God is speaking to us! Hear him! Obey him!" That, in essence, is the appeal which this writer evidently feels it necessary to repeat time and time again in this epistle.

Here, it is intensified and reinforced by the solemn reminder of a tragic historic precedent. Of all the warnings in Hebrews, that in chapters 3 and 4 is the most extended and the most explicit. We can only look now briefly at some of its main points as they throw light on the warning in chapter 6 on which this study is mainly based.

We should note:

1. The Kadesh-Barnea rebellion, and God's subsequent judgment of the rebels, is accepted by the writer as a significant event in the history of God's covenant people, Israel.

2. David's warning to his own generation, four hundred years later, having been based on the event, the writer assumes that this is a valid precedent for its application as a basis of his warning to his New Covenant brethren in the first century AD.

3. On the basis of this (and other) Old Testament precedents, the writer asserts that membership of "God's house" (3:6), "sharing in Christ" (3:14), and entrance into "God's rest" (4:1ff), are the heritage of the saints under the New Covenant. They are to be secured by a firm continuance in the faith, but can be forfeited by disobedience and unbelief (3:6, 12–14; 4:11, etc).

4. Attention is given particularly to the reference in Psalm 95 to "God's rest", and to entrance into that "rest".

On this last point, we should note that the writer is concerned to point out that David, in his reference to "God's rest", must have been looking at a condition or event beyond the conquest of the Promised Land: "For if Joshua had given them rest, God would not speak later [that is, through David] of another day" (4:8). In fact, the writer is now introducing another important detail of his main theme. He continues (verse 9): "So then, there remains a sabbath rest ("sabbatismos") for the people of God; for whoever enters God's rest also ceases from his labours as God did from his."

This "sabbath rest", he clearly implies, is still future. So it is not that inner rest of spirit which the Christian may experience when his mind is stayed wholly on the Lord, though that is no doubt a foretaste of it. The writer is speaking about a sabbath rest which "remains"; in other words, a rest which has yet to be entered into, and which he urges his readers to "strive to enter" (3:11). Interestingly too, he implies that the "good news" of that future rest had also been available to the godly of David's day, before the coming of Christ. (4:2, 8–9).

This comes out clearly in Hebrews 11, where the writer speaks of Abraham and Moses, and other men and women of faith in the former age who: "died in faith, not having received what was promised, but having seen it and greeted it from afar". "All these", he says, as he concludes that passage (11:39), "though well attested by their faith, did not receive what was promised, since God had foreseen something better for us that apart from us, they should not be made perfect."

It hardly need be said that the writer is not here implying that those Old Covenant saints will fail to receive the reward of their faith (and faithfulness). What he says is that they will not enter into the promised inheritance (or "rest") until the full complement of New Covenant participators has been made up.

The reference throughout, it should be noted, is to *"God's rest"*, which is specifically referred to as a "sabbath rest", or "sabbatismos" [the only place in the NT where that word is found]. A sabbath rest is a "rest period", taken in the course of a period of labour. It both follows and precedes periods of work. The writer draws attention to the fact that God took such a "rest" when he had completed the work of creation: "And God rested on the seventh day from all his works" (4:4). This cannot therefore be a reference to that "eternal rest", outside of time, in which God dwells eternally.

God's "sabbath rest" after the completion of his work of creation ceased when man fell into sin. Thereafter he entered into the work of redemption and restoration. This necessitated his sending his Son into the world "to make purification for sins" (Hebrews 1:3). The Father and the Son moved together in perfect unity in the accomplishment of this great work. "My Father is working still, and I am working," Jesus revealed to the Jews (John 5:17). Ahead of him at that time was the crucifixion, that great central feature of his ongoing "work". Jesus, now risen and glorified, sits enthroned at the Father's right hand, and, in fellowship with the Father, the work continues as Jesus engages ceaselessly in his high priestly ministry on behalf of the "sons" with whom he intends to share his kingdom.

Then, when the age-long conflict with the powers of darkness will have climaxed in a decisive victory for Christ, "the kingdom of the world (will) become the kingdom of our Lord and of his Christ" (Revelation 11:15). Thus will be inaugurated the "sabbath rest" of God, when the Father will have committed the government of heaven and earth to the Son. (Psalm 110:1; Hebrews 1:13; Matthew 22:44).

Into that "rest" the covenant people are invited to enter; indeed, it is their inheritance. But it is by no means a foregone conclusion that all those invited to share this privilege will do so, otherwise there would be no point in the warning which accompanies this new sidelight on the "kingdom" theme.

We should note that this theme of "God's rest" is introduced with the reference to the building of "God's house" (3:1ff). In Acts 7, where Luke gives an extensive account of Stephen's defence of his faith, Stephen is reported as quoting from Isaiah 66:

> The Most High does not dwell in houses
> made with hands; as the prophet says,
> 'Heaven is my throne, and earth my footstool.
> What house will you build for me, says the Lord,
> or what is the place of my rest?
> Did not my hands make all these things?'

God does not dwell in houses made with hands. Rather, as our writer implies, he will establish his household (or resting-place) among those of his redeemed people who "hold fast their confidence and pride in their hope firm to the end" (3:6). "What is the house which you would build for me," says the Lord, "and what is the place of my rest?" ... His word through the prophet continues: "But this is the man to whom I will look, he that is humble and contrite in spirit, and trembles at my word" (Isaiah 66:1,2).

This brings us back to the concluding words of this second warning. Hebrews 4:10 reads: "for whoever enters God's rest also ceases from his labours as God did from his."

This verse is often misunderstood. The writer is *not* saying: "Whoever enters God's rest (now) also ceases (now) from his labours as God did from his." That would be an illogical interpretation in the light of all the writer has just been saying. God did not enter *his* rest until he had ceased from his work. Nor can we enter our rest until we have finished our earthly course. This is made doubly clear by the exhortation which follows. We are to "strive to enter that rest, that no one fall by the same sort of disobedience" (11)—the same sort, that is, as that of the children of Israel when they were journeying to the Promised Land. They lacked that trust, that humble and contrite spirit, and that awesome respect for the Lord, that causes men to "tremble at (his) word". "For", as our writer says in the conclusion of this warning:

> ... the word of God is living and active, sharper than any two-edged sword, piercing to the division of soul and spirit, of joints and marrow, and discerning the thoughts and intentions of the heart. And before him no creature is hidden, but all are open and laid bare to the eyes of him with whom we have to do (4:12,13).

With those solemn reminders he concludes his second warning which provides the key to an understanding of the one which is to follow in chapter 6. We shall return to that warning in the next chapter.

CHAPTER SIX

The Warning of Apostasy

WHEN THIS EPISTLE WAS FIRST DELIVERED TO THE CHRISTIAN community for which it was originally intended, presumably it would have come into the hands of one of its leaders. Having read it through, and grasped something of its immense importance, he would have taken an early opportunity to gather his brethren together to read it to them.

It would not then have been divided into chapters and verses as we have it today, so there would have been no inducement to read it piecemeal. We may suppose therefore that it would have been read through at one sitting, as letters are usually read. Allowing for pauses here and there for explanation or comment, this would probably have taken about an hour. During the reading, the hearers—if indeed they were "hearing" what was being read—would have got a pretty good grasp of the main thrust of the message; better, one suspects, than many of us do nowadays, after years of attention to individual chapters or passages, rather than to the epistle as a whole.

Hebrews is made up of two interwoven strands, rather like the strands of an electric cable: one being "positive", the other "negative". Both are necessary to convey the light, heat, and power of its great message.

It begins with the "positive" revelation of the Son through whom God "in these last days" is speaking to us. Then the "negative" strand briefly appears. To hear the word of God is a solemn responsibility, especially when those to whom he speaks are "heirs of salvation". And so it is in that connection that the writer introduces his first warning: "How shall we escape if we neglect such a great salvation?" (2:3).

This leads on to the introduction of "Jesus" as the "pioneer" (or author) of their salvation" (2:10). He had already been introduced as "the Son of God"; but now, in connection with the work of "making purification for sins", and in order that he might become "a merciful and faithful high priest" on their behalf, "he had to be made like his brethren in every respect" (2:17). That was why it became necessary for him to partake of human nature and human flesh, and to adopt a human name.

Then comes the second warning (chapters 3 and 4), which we considered in our last chapter. "Great salvation"—in terms of the possession of "the land flowing with milk and honey"—had been offered to Israel by way of an inheritance. But most of them had "fallen away", and so forfeited their right of possession. The warning therefore concludes with the exhortation: "Let us strive to enter God's rest, that no one fall by the same sort of disobedience" (4:11).

After this warning the writer again takes up the "positive" theme of the high priestly ministry of Jesus: "Since then we have a great high priest who has passed through the heavens, Jesus, the Son of God, let us hold fast our confession. For we have not a high priest who is unable to sympathize with our weaknesses, but one who in every respect has been tempted as we are, yet without sin" (4:14).

Pursuing this theme, he now turns again to Psalm 110 which he had quoted in chapter one when he had sought to establish, on the authority of Scripture, the Son's superiority over angels. Now, however, he draws attention to the later reference in the psalm in which the triumphant and exalted "Lord" at God's right hand is also designated "a priest for ever after the order of Melchizedek". That, as the writer will take care to explain later, is a very high order of priesthood indeed, higher, not only than that of the sons of Levi, of which Moses was the outstanding representative, but also of the great patriarch Abraham, "the friend of God". The writer longs to share with these brethren the implications of this prophecy. But, as we have seen, he breaks off from the development of his theme because he doubts whether they are yet ready to receive his word.

At Hebrews 5:11, therefore, the negative strand reappears. Having admonished his readers for their dullness of hearing, and consequent immaturity, he exhorts them to "go on to maturity"; adding (hopefully), "and this we will do, if God permits". Yet, instead of taking up the threads of his main

The Warning of Apostasy

theme, he now plunges into this further warning. Why should he do this? His readers should still have had his earlier warnings on their minds. Did he then have some misgivings as to whether he had sufficiently clarified the implications of that Old Testament warning for these New Testament saints?

David, in Psalm 95, in exhorting his own generation, had drawn attention to God's judgment upon their forefathers as a nation, on account of their unbelief and rebellion. But God had made it clear through the prophet Jeremiah (Jeremiah 31:33–34) that under the terms of a New Covenant he would establish a personal relationship with his covenant people. He would put his law within them, and write it upon their hearts. "I will be their God," he said, "and they shall be my people. And no longer shall each man teach his neighbour and each his brother, saying, 'Know the LORD', for they shall all know me, from the least to the greatest . . .".

So far, therefore, from David's exhortation being regarded as no longer appropriate, the conditions of the New Covenant placed on them an even greater responsibility to make a personal response to the word of God. That is the burden of Hebrews throughout. "God . . . in these last days has spoken to us in his Son" . . . "we must pay the closer attention . . ." . . . "Today . . . hear his voice . . ." . . . "see that you refuse not him who is speaking". Such exhortations come time and time again throughout the epistle.

That is why a closer examination of the Kadesh-Barnea crisis was called for, and also, a more specific explanation of the nature of "rebellion" in relation to "Jesus, the Son of God", through whom God now speaks to us.

This is what the writer determines he must bring to his reader's attention before he resumes the development of the theme of the Melchizedek priesthood.

The connection between this warning and the two preceding ones is evident. The first one urged the importance of "giving closer attention to what we have heard, lest we drift away from it" (like a boat that slips anchor and drifts out to sea). The second one, based on the Kadesh-Barnea rebellion, elaborates on that brief earlier statement, and concludes with the exhortation: "Take care, brethren, lest there be in any of you an evil unbelieving heart, leading you to fall away from the living God" (3:12). In this further warning, the same dreaded symptoms are again in view. The danger is still, in effect, drift, slipping anchor, losing contact.

The wording of the passage is somewhat difficult, and the full implications of what is clearly intended to be a very deliberate statement is by no means obvious, especially if the passage is read out of context. It may help, therefore, if we examine it under three headings: (1) The class of people in view. (2) The condition of heart of which they have to beware. (3) The consequences which could result from that condition.

1. The class of people in view.

The writer is careful to identify them by five characteristics: (i) They had been enlightened. (ii) They had tasted the heavenly gift. (iii) They had become partakers of the Holy Spirit. (iv) They had tasted the goodness of the word of God. (v) They had tasted the powers of the age to come.

Not forgetting that we are considering a message addressed to New Covenant believers, we will first consider in what ways these characteristics applied to the people of Israel whose conduct—or misconduct—had been a central feature of the earlier warning.

(i) They had been enlightened.

God had covenanted with Abraham that his seed should become a great nation whom he would bless, and in whom all nations of the earth would be blessed. Yet Abraham's descendants through Jacob began their history as a nation in a strange land under heathen rulers. Initially they multiplied and prospered. Gradually however they lost touch with the God of their fathers—Jehovah, "the living and true God". Eventually they were reduced to cruel servitude under one of the later Pharoahs. Yet God did not forget his covenant, but raised up Moses to be the deliverer of his people. Moses's first task was to enlighten his fellow-countrymen concerning "the God of their fathers", for they did not even know his name. They needed also to be enlightened as to the fact that they were his chosen people ("my people": Exodus 3:7), and that his purpose was to bring them into "a good and broad land, a land flowing with milk and honey".

The New Testament saints to whom Hebrews was sent were also referred to as having been "enlightened" (10:32). Their enlightenment had been centred in the person of Jesus—"God manifested in flesh"—and in their call to be involved in his kingdom purposes.

(ii) They had tasted the heavenly gift.

When God's people set out on their pilgrimage to the Promised Land, he fed them with "manna". In John 6, Jesus refers to this as "the bread of heaven", and says further:

> My Father gives you the true bread from heaven. For the bread of God is that which came down from heaven, and gives life to the world ... I am the living bread which came down from heaven; if any one eats of this bread, he will live for ever; and the bread which I shall give for the life of the world is my flesh (John 6:32,51).

The Lord's unfailing availability as "the living bread" is powerfully symbolized in the sacrament of "the breaking of the bread" which he instituted "in remembrance of me".

(iii) They had become partakers of the Holy Spirit.

Coming to Horeb, Moses is told by the Lord: "You shall strike the rock, and water shall come out of it, that the people may drink".

Water is frequently the symbol of the Holy Spirit in Scripture. In John 7, Jesus is quoted as saying:

> If any one thirst, let him come to me and drink. He who believes in me, as the scripture has said, "Out of his heart shall flow rivers of living water." Now this he said about the Spirit, which those who believed in him were to receive (John 7:37–39).

The application Paul draws from the gifts both of the manna and the water from the rock should also be noticed:

(our fathers) all ate the same supernatural food and all drank the same supernatural drink. For they drank from the supernatural Rock which followed them, and the Rock was Christ (1 Cor. 10:3,4).

Nor should we forget that invitation of "the Spirit and the Bride" in the closing sentences of the Revelation: "Let him who is thirsty come (and) take the water of life without price" (Revelation 22:17).

First, the manna from heaven, then the water from the smitten rock. First Christ, the living bread from heaven (John 6:51), then the Spirit who is "the water of life" (John 7:38). First Calvary, then Pentecost. The divine order of these events should be carefully noted.

(iv) They had tasted the goodness of the word of God.

The Israelites journeyed on from Horeb to Sinai, where the law of God, written on two tables of stone, was given to them. The word was "good". It was intended to be a way of life, not death. The godly of that age would echo the words of the psalmist: "Oh, how I love thy law! It is my meditation all the day" (Psalm 119:97). Paul, in a later age, could speak similarly: "the law is holy, and the commandment is holy and just and good" (Romans 7:12). As we have seen, our writer had spoken of his brethren's need to be taught again "the first principles of God's word", and had referred to "the elementary doctrine of Christ" (Hebrews 5:12, 6:1). Furthermore, in New Covenant language, the term "the word of God" had acquired a new significance. For Jesus, as the incarnate Son of God, is "the Word made flesh"—the living expression of the thoughts of God, the one through whom God now speaks to us.

(v) They had tasted the powers of the age to come.

Throughout their years of wandering in the wilderness, God's presence among his earthly people was evidenced by supernatural happenings. They were accompanied by the pillar of cloud by day and of fire by night; by miracles of divine protection and provision, and, at times, of chastisement.

The Warning of Apostasy

This had also been true in the experience of these New Covenant Christians. The Gospel of the Kingdom ("great salvation") which had been declared at first by the Lord, and which they had received, had been borne witness to "by signs and wonders and various miracles and by gifts of the Holy Spirit distributed according to [God's] will" (Hebrews 2:4).

So too, throughout the whole of the Christian era, many of those who have walked with God have "tasted of the powers of the age to come". Such signs and wonders are foretastes of the glory of the coming kingdom. There are prophetic scriptures which suggest that as we come nearer to that coming age, we should expect to see increasing evidence of such signs. [eg: Joel 2, with Acts 2:17–20]

The Christians who received this message would have had no difficulty in realizing that all these things were true of them and of other Christians of that time. Nor, one suspects, would they have had any difficulty in relating what they now heard to the warning which preceded it, which had been based on the familiar story of Israel's rebellion at Kadesh-Barnea. Although the writer makes no actual reference here to that event, the implications would have been self-evident.

2. The condition of heart of which they are to beware.

The writer has in view nothing less than "apostasy"—a falling away from the living God [see 3:12]. The language is specific and forceful. It is in this connection that we need particularly to relate back to the historic precedent provided in the previous warning.

Encamped at Kadesh-Barnea the people of Israel were almost within sight of the Promised Land. Behind them was a wonderful experience of God's providence. They had been brought out of bondage in Egypt. They had been provisioned, protected, instructed, and empowered. They had experienced foretastes of coming glory. Not least, they had known the constant forbearance of the Lord in spite of their persistent disobedience and complainings.

Now was their day of testing. Moses had sent twelve men to spy out Canaan in anticipation of the whole nation going up to possess it. These men all duly returned. Two of them, Caleb and Joshua, brought an encouraging report: "Let us go up at once and occupy it; for we are well able to overcome it." The remaining ten, however, vigorously opposed this verdict: "We are not able to go up against the people; for they are stronger than we" (Numbers 13:30, 31).

It was the language of faith versus the language of unbelief; and, sadly, it was the language of unbelief which prevailed with the people, for in heart they had already fallen away from the Lord.

Yet we should remember they were still the chosen people of God; the favoured nation with whom he had entered into a covenant of blessing; a people who had experienced his goodness and power; who had received his firm promise of safe passage into the land promised to them for an inheritance. Yet they "fell away"; "All the people of Israel murmured against Moses and Aaron . . . 'Would God we had died in Egypt . . . or in the wilderness!'" (Numbers 14:2). In effect, they were saying: "Would God we had never been redeemed!" In language which our writer will use later in the epistle (10:29): "[they] profaned the blood of the covenant by which [they were] sanctified, and outraged the Spirit of grace."

That was the measure of their apostasy; and although the Son of God had not yet been manifested in flesh, so that their rebellion was not consciously against him, yet in heart they were a kind of archetype of those in this age who, as the writer says, "crucify the Son of God on their own account, and hold him up to contempt" (6:6). It is against such a degree of apostasy that the writer warns his brethren, and us. We may question our need to be warned in this manner, but such complacency could be dangerous. From the passage which follows it is evident that these Hebrew Christians had in earlier days been strong in their faith and their commitment to the Lord. Yet the writer evidently feels it necessary to warn them in these terms. "Take care, brethren, lest there be in any of *you* an evil, unbelieving heart, leading you to fall away from the living God" (3:12).

The matter that had brought things to a head at Kadesh-

Barnea was the challenge of what was involved in claiming the promised inheritance. Many Christians, in these days, are never seriously challenged in such a way, for they have never understood "salvation" other than in terms which imply that the inheritance is an integral part of redemption and is non-forfeitable. This is mainly because most evangelical teaching emphasizes only the *grace* of God in relation to salvation by faith, and refers in only the vaguest terms to the possibility of "loss" consequent on disobedience.

3. The consequence of apostasy.

In the account of Numbers 14, Moses pleads with God not to destroy his people, and God answers Moses:

> I have pardoned, according to your word; but truly, as I live, and as all the earth shall be filled with the glory of the LORD, none of the men who have seen my glory and my signs which I wrought in Egypt and in the wilderness, and yet have put me to the proof these ten times and have not hearkened to my voice, shall see the land which I swore to give to their fathers; and none of those who despised me shall see it.

We should note: (i) The Lord pardoned his people. The rebels had cried: "Would God we had died in Egypt!", and had even proposed choosing a captain to lead them back to the land of their captivity. But God in his mercy would not permit them to do what, in effect, would have amounted to a reversal of their redemption experience. Their redemption from Egypt was not forfeitable; for that had been God's work alone, without any effort or merit on their part.

(ii) But, as far as the inheritance was concerned, they had shot their bolt. The inheritance had to be claimed, and at Kadesh-Barnea the rebels had clearly indicated their refusal to go up and possess it. For a long time the Lord had borne patiently with them. But there comes a point when his Spirit will no longer strive with the rebellious heart. In response to Moses's intervention they were pardoned. God would not permit their return to Egypt. But neither were they permitted to enter the land of their inheritance. Their own death-wish, uttered in rebellion, was to be fulfilled.

They had sealed their own destiny. That was God's final judgment on that rebellious generation of his covenant people; and it was unalterable. When Moses told them of this, they "mourned greatly". That, however, was only because the reality of the consequences of their sin had come home to their hearts at last. There was no real repentance. On the contrary, it was in open defiance of the Lord's command that "they presumed to go up to the heights of the hill country, although neither the ark of the covenant of the LORD, nor Moses, departed out of the camp". On their lips, as they went, were the pious words: "We will go up to the place which the LORD has promised; for we have sinned." But the Lord was no longer with them. Inevitably, they were quickly routed by the Amalekites and Caananites who occupied the land.

God's purpose in redeeming his people was not only to deliver them from bondage but that he might bring them into their glorious inheritance. This was a two-stage operation. In the same way, in the accomplishment of the "great salvation" which he desires for his New Covenant people there are two distinct stages. Redemption is his work alone. God had said to his people in Egypt: "When I see the blood"—the blood of atonement sprinkled on the two sideposts and lintel of their doors—"I will pass over you." It was the blood alone which provided protection on the night of judgment. In the same way, it is the precious blood of Jesus alone which now gives his people the assurance of deliverance from guilt and access into his presence without fear.

But entrance into "the inheritance of the saints" is still conditional upon obedience. Between Egypt and Canaan lay the wilderness. Israel's journey through the wilderness provided opportunity, not only to prove the faithfulness of their Lord, but also to test theirs. Never for one moment did the Lord fail them through their journeyings. But they proved faithless; and a whole generation (with one or two exceptions) forfeited their inheritance.

When did this tragic story of Israel's backsliding begin to develop? It was not on the night of the Passover; nor on that memorable day when by divine intervention they crossed the Red Sea on dry land. But gradually, it would seem, they

The Warning of Apostasy

became more and more preoccupied with their immediate affairs and circumstances; the vision of the inheritance faded; their hearts grew cold; their faith ebbed away. They came to accept the continuing, unfailing providence of the Lord as of right.

Backsliding is a gradual process, a consequence of the exposure of the mind to evil, whether through direct contact with the world, or through satanic influence, or out of what the writer earlier referred to as "an evil, unbelieving heart". It is not inevitable, but the risk is there; and, as those of us who have lived into the later years of life know, temptation can strike at any time. These Hebrew Christians were not novices. In fact, when later the writer refers to their earlier days he reminds them of how they had "endured a hard struggle with sufferings". They had joyfully accepted the plundering of their property, since (they) knew that (they) had a better possession and an abiding one". Furthermore, he confidently expresses the conviction that, in their case "better things that belong to salvation" were to be expected (verse 9).

Why then should he warn them in this way? It was because they had evidently been drifting, and the possibility of further backsliding, leading even to apostasy, was a risk they could not afford to ignore. He was far from believing they had reached the point of no return; indeed his hope, even expectation, was that they would now heed his exhortation and "go on to maturity".

There are degrees of backsliding, and only the Lord knows when anyone has reached that point from which no further recovery is possible. One has known of cases where, after years of apparent rejection of the Lord, people have returned to him in true repentance. Yet the warning is here, and none of us can afford to disregard it.

It is noticeable that in bringing this warning, the writer extends the scope of his readership as he refers to "*those* who have once been enlightened"; "if *they* then commit apostasy"; "*they* crucify the Son of God on their own account". This could be because he is aware that he is in fact writing for a much wider circle than the company to whom the epistle was originally sent. Under the direction of the Holy Spirit his message is to become an essential part of "the oracles of God" for all the people of God in this New Covenant age.

No servant of Christ was more aware of the need of such warnings than the apostle Paul. He was under no illusion that the call he had personally received on the Damascus road constituted a guarantee for him of a place of honour in the kingdom of God's Son. Writing to the Corinthians he says:

> Do you not know that in a race all the runners compete, but only one receives the prize? So run that you may obtain it. Every athlete exercises self-control in all things. They do it to receive a perishable wreath, but we an imperishable. Well, I do not run aimlessly, I do not box as one beating the air; but I pommel my body and subdue it, lest after preaching to others I myself should be disqualified (1 Corinthians 9:24–27).

"I pommel my body and subdue it" surely implies a continuing daily discipline which Paul accepted as essential training in order that he might qualify to "receive the prize".

Using a similar analogy, he lays his heart bare to the Christians at Philippi when he testifies:

> I count everything as loss because of the surpassing worth of knowing Christ Jesus my Lord. For his sake I have suffered the loss of all things, and count them as refuse, in order that I may gain Christ . . . . (Philippians 3:8).

What we have here is not a man's "religious beliefs", but his testimony to the faith by which he lives. It is as realistic as the profit and loss account of a trading concern. On the "loss" side is everything which, before he met Jesus on the Damascus road, he had counted dear. On the "profit" side is "the surpassing worth of knowing Christ". If we could ask Paul: "How's business?" his answer might have been: "We're doing fine, thanks!" "I rejoice in the Lord greatly" he says. "I can do all things in him who strengthens me"; "I have received full payment, and more". And, for full measure, he will conclude: "And my God shall supply every need of yours according to his riches in glory in Christ Jesus" (Philippians 4:10–19). So, in spite of the huge sacri-

The Warning of Apostasy

fices he had appeared to make when he came "under new management", Paul's "business" was now, on his testimony "a flourishing concern". But even so, he was not complacent. He still entertains ambitions for further spiritual advance:

> that I may know him and the power of his resurrection, and may share his sufferings, becoming like him in his death, that if possible I may attain the resurrection from the dead (Philippians 3:10).

Paul is in no doubt that the experience of the power of Christ's resurrection in one's life is inevitably bound up with participation in his sufferings. Nor does he assume that, for him, the "prize" has yet been secured; for he goes on to say:

> Not that I have already obtained this or am already perfect; but I press on to make it my own, because Christ Jesus has made me his own ... but one thing I do, forgetting what lies behind .... I press on toward the goal for the prize of the upward call of God in Christ Jesus (Philippians 3:12–14).

In connection with our present study, we do well to consider the implications of these two fragments of self-revelation by the great apostle to the Gentiles. Both are addressed to predominently Gentile Christian communities. Yet they perfectly echo the spirit and emphasis of the Hebrew epistle, both with regard to the great objective "hope of salvation", and to what is involved in the noble endeavour to be "made worthy of the kingdom of God" (2 Thes. 1:5).

How many of us can truly echo Paul's words: "This one thing I do ... I press on toward the goal for the prize of the upward call in Christ Jesus"? What makes Paul's ministry so challenging to our hearts is the knowledge that what he preached to others he honestly endeavoured to practise personally.

We come now to the writer's footnote to his third warning:

> For land which has drunk the rain that often falls upon it, and brings forth vegetation useful to those for whose sake it is cultivated, receives a blessing from God. But if it bears thorns and thistles, it is worthless and near to being cursed; its end is to be burned (Hebrews 6:7–8).

We noted earlier (see chapter 3) the points of comparison between this passage and that in 1 Corinthians 3 where Paul deals with the question of what is to be built on the one foundation which is Christ Jesus. Here (Hebrews 6), the analogy is not of building, but of the cultivation of land. Under normal conditions, land produces growth, and cultivated land "brings forth vegetation useful to those for whose sake it is cultivated". Uncultivated land, however, often produces thorns and thistles. Such land is said to be "worthless and near to being cursed". "Its end is to be burned", and that, paradoxically, is its salvation. For what the fire destroys is not the land itself, but its worthless and dishonouring product. The consequence is similar to that which Paul has in view in the building analogy in 1 Corinthians 3 where he concludes: "If any man's work is burned up, he will suffer loss, though he himself will be saved, but only through fire" (3:14).

"You are God's field, God' building", Paul says (3:9). So whichever analogy is used, the character of what is produced is of supreme importance. Those who build with shoddy materials will suffer loss. The worthless product of "God's field", will be reduced to ashes. There will be no argument, no court of appeal. It will be tried by fire. "The Day will disclose it" (3:13).

But the land itself escapes final judgment. It is nigh to being cursed; but it is not cursed. "God's firm foundation stands, bearing this seal: 'The Lord knows who are his,' and 'Let every one who names the name of the Lord depart from iniquity'" (2 Timothy 2:19).

God claimed as his own special people those whom he brought out of Egypt. No power in heaven or hell or on earth can deny or destroy that which God has decreed or accomplished. His firm foundation stands. He knows them that are his. But there are two sides to the seal. It is good that we are able to "name the name of the Lord". That, however, is not enough. Those who would enter the land, who would gain the prize of the upward calling of God in Christ Jesus, are those who "depart from iniquity"; those who build in Christ's kingdom with the materials which he supplies; those whose cultivated ground produces useful vegetation. The Day will declare it!

The Warning of Apostasy

One further point in this passage in Hebrews 6 which remains to be considered is the significance of the word "impossible" with which the passage is introduced. Speaking of those who have enjoyed the benefits of God's providence, he says that "it is impossible to restore [them] again to repentance . . . if they then commit apostasy . . ." This unqualified assertion of "impossibility" has puzzled many Christians. When (in verse 18) the writer says: "It is impossible that God should prove false," that presents no problem. Used here, however, it seems to imply that, even in this life, a backslider may reach a point from which there is no possibility of recovery.

Looking at this warning in conjunction with the earlier one (in chapters 3 and 4) based on the historic precedent of the Kadesh-Barnea rebellion, that inference seems irresistible. God loved the Old Covenant people just as much as he loves us; yet he had to say: "I have pardoned . . . . but truly, as I live, and as all the earth shall be filled with the glory of the LORD, none of the men who have seen my glory . . . and have not hearkened to my voice, shall see the land which I swore to give to their fathers . . .". He is the same God who is speaking to us today—in his word, and in his Son who is "the word made flesh".

Many Christians have difficulty in reconciling this passage with the doctrine of the eternal security of the believer; and rather than that the doctrine should be threatened it has been argued that these warning passages are not applicable to "born again" Christians, but only to mere "professors" of Christianity. I hope, however, that our consideration of many passages in Hebrews, along with many other relevant scriptures, suffices to show that these warnings are entirely consistent with the Gospel of the Kingdom which Jesus taught and commanded his disciples to teach to Jew and Gentile alike. "They were written down for our instruction, upon whom the end of the ages has come" (1 Corinthians 10:11).

One of the few other places where this word "impossible" is found is in one of the "kingdom" parables which the Lord used in speaking to his disciples. He said: "Children, how hard it is to enter the kingdom of God! It is easier for a camel to go through the eye of a needle than for a rich man to enter the kingdom of God." At these words, Mark tells us, his disciples were "exceedingly astonished, and said to him, 'Then who can be saved?' Jesus looked at them and said: 'With men, it is impossible, but not with God; for all things are possible with God'" (Mark 10:23–31).

Important though the teaching of this parable is in relation to the theme of Hebrews, it must suffice now simply to recognize that it was from the lips of the Lord himself that those encouraging words fell: "for all things are possible with God".

The God who warns us of the consequences of disobedience is a God of infinite compassion. In Jesus, he has provided a great high priest who sympathizes with our weaknesses; who provides us with all needed strength to overcome, and gives us strong encourgement to "seize the hope that is set before us".

It is that "strong encouragement" which the write is now determined to give to his beloved brethren, and it is this to which we shall be giving consideration in our next chapter.

Chapter Seven

Strong Encouragement

HEBREWS HAS BEEN DESCRIBED AS "THE EPISTLE OF WARNING", but this gives an unbalanced impression of the essential character of this great book. It does contain warnings—five altogether—but its main theme is the high priestly ministry of the Lord Jesus, and that is essentially one of encouragement.

Facing the dark realities of the satanic system, and of sin and temptation, Hebrews unfolds in a unique way the mystery of God's provision in Jesus whereby his New Covenant people may live victoriously and so claim their inheritance.

In the passage we have been considering (Hebrews 5 and 6) an admonitory note has been sounded, warning the readers of the danger and consequences of apostasy. Without retracting one word of this, the writer now changes his tone to one of encouragement as a lead-in to the resumption of his main theme.

"Though we speak thus, yet in your case, beloved, we feel sure of better things that belong to salvation," he says (6:9). Is he indulging here in a bit of mild flattery in an attempt to coax these brethren out of their sluggishness? Perhaps so. Yet it is clear that he still has confidence in them, and he now gives his reasons for this (6:10):

> For God is not so unjust as to overlook your work and the love which you showed for his sake in serving the saints, as you still do.

So the ground of his confidence is the conviction that God will take account of *their* work and *their* love for his sake, in serving the saints. He continues (6:11,12):

> And we desire each one of you to show the same earnestness in realizing the full assurance of hope until the end, so that you may not be sluggish, but imitators of those who through faith and patience inherit the promises.

This can mean only that those for whom these words are intended have a "hope"—in fact, a "promise"—the fulfilment of which is conditional. There is need for the continuance of "the same earnestness" which had marked them formerly. Those who will "inherit the promises", are those whose lives are characterized, not by faith alone, but by "faith *and* patience".

How does this match up with Paul's emphatic statement (Ephesians 2:8): "For by grace you have been saved through faith; and this is not your own doing, it is the gift of God—not because of works, lest any man should boast"?

There is no conflict. In Ephesians 2 Paul is looking at the foundational truth of justification, which is on the basis of faith in the sacrificial work of Christ alone. Here, in Hebrews, it is the inheritance of the Kingdom which is in view. Later in Ephesians Paul also takes up the same theme of the Kingdom in words which are fully in accord with the message of Hebrews: "Be sure of this, that no fornicator or impure man, or one who is covetous (that is an idolator), has any inheritance in the kingdom of Christ and of God" (Ephesians 5:5).

As an outstanding example of those who are to be imitated, our writer now draws attention to Abraham. We are reminded that when God promised Abraham "Surely I will bless you and multiply you", he confirmed it with an oath (6:13, 14). But was not Abraham unique as the founding father of the chosen nation of Israel; and do we not live in an entirely different social environment at the end of this twentieth century AD? How then can we be expected to derive personal encouragement from Abraham's story? The answer to that question will emerge as we look carefully at this passage.

First, we should note that in the many references to Abraham in the New Testament the focus of attention is not on his "founding father" role, but on his faith. "Abraham believed God" (Romans 4:3). This is why, as Paul says (Galatians 3:6,7), he is reckoned as the father of all men of faith. "There is neither Jew nor Greek . . . for you are all one in Christ Jesus. And if you are Christ's, then you are Abraham's offspring, heirs according to promise" (Galatians 3:28,29).

Strong Encouragement

Then we should note what emerges out of the writer's statement that the promise God made to Abraham had been confirmed by an oath. "An oath is final for confirmation", he adds, and then goes on to say (6:17,18):

> So when God desired to show more convincingly to the heirs of the promise the unchangeable character of his purpose, he (confirmed it) with an oath, so that through two unchangeable things, in which it is impossible that God should prove false, we who have fled for refuge might have strong encouragement to seize the hope set before us.

Who are the "heirs of promise"? They would presumably include all in every age with whom God has entered into a covenant of promise. But there can be little question that God's New Covenant people are particularly in the writer's mind, including those to whom this epistle was originally addressed. For, as he says, it is *"we* who ... have strong encouragement to seize the hope set before us".

So it is to "the heirs of the promise" within the terms of the New Covenant that God desires to show "the unchangeable character of his purpose". As to what that "purpose" is, it is clearly revealed in the earlier chapters of this epistle that it is the bringing to glory of the "many sons" made like his unique Son (Hebrews 2:10ff). That was the divine purpose from before the foundation of the world (Ephesians 1:4). It was the impelling purpose in the heart of Jesus as he dwelt among us in the days of his flesh; and it is his purpose still as, in his risen glory, he continues to exercise his high priestly ministry on our behalf in the presence of his Father.

To what then is the writer referring when he speaks here of God's oath to the heirs of promise? Earlier (5:5,6) he introduced two quotations from the psalms, the second of these being from Psalm 110: "Thou art a priest for ever, after the order of Melchizedek." Looking at this statement in the context of Psalm 110, we find that it is introduced with the words: "The LORD has sworn and will not change his mind ...". It is to this oath that the writer now refers.

Psalm 110 is the messianic psalm which begins with the prophetic words: "Sit at my right hand until I make your enemies your footstool." These words are now applied in

Hebrews to "Jesus, the Son of God" [see Hebrews 1:13 with 4:14]. They present Jesus as seated at the Father's right hand until the time comes when he will be enthroned as "King of kings and Lord of lords".

The oath is given in relation to his priestly, rather than his kingly, role. He is appointed to an eternal, unchanging priesthood "after the order of Melchizedek". It is concerning that priestly ministry that our writer has much to say "which is hard to explain". What he is saying in these closing sentences in Hebrews 6 is in preparation for a resumption of that theme. In Hebrews 7 he will be careful to point out that in Melchizedek the two roles—of king and high priest—were merged into one; he is both "king of Salem" and "priest of the Most High God". And he has this further to say:

> He is first, by translation of his name, king of righteousness, and then he is also king of Salem, that is, king of peace. He is without father or mother or genealogy, and has neither beginning of days nor end of life, but resembling the Son of God he continues a priest for ever (Hebrews 7:2,3).

"See how great he is!" he exclaims in summing up this brief biography of Melchizedek: "for (even) Abraham the patriarch gave him a tithe of the spoils" (7:4).

What is the significance of this for us?

It is that, in Jesus, God has fulfilled his promise concerning the appointment of "a high priest after the order of Melchizedek". In fact, Melchizedek becomes a mere shadow as the Son of God, who having appeared in human flesh and taken to himself the human name of Jesus, is revealed as the person in whom the promise of Psalm 110 has been fulfilled. Jesus is "the apostle and high priest of *our* confession" (3:1). He is a priest, "not according to a legal requirement . . . but by the power of an indestructible life" (7:16). As such, he exercises "a ministry which is as much more excellent than the old as the covenant he mediates is better, since it is enacted on better promises" (8:6). Because he holds his priesthood permanently "he is able for all time to save those who draw near to God through him, since he always lives to make intercession for them" (7: 24, 25).

Abraham, as the "father of us all" (Romans 4:16)—that is, as our pioneer in the pathway of faith—"patiently endured" and "obtained the promise". For us, all that was implicit in the Melchizedek priesthood has been revealed and made available in Jesus, so that we too may patiently endure and obtain the promise. It is on the basis of this glorious revelation of the high priestly ministry of the Lord Jesus that the writer speaks of the "strong encouragement" which is given to us—"the heirs of promise"—"to seize the hope set before us".

Let us then again be reminded of what the writer has in mind when he speaks of that "hope".

The reference in Hebrews 3:6 to "our pride in our hope" introduced the second warning with its lessons based on the story of the Israelites' rebellion at Kadesh-Barnea and their consequent failure to enter the Promised Land. In the chapter we are considering, there is the reference to "realizing the full assurance of hope until the end" (6:11). It is the hope of the inheritance which is in view; the hope which has been placed within our reach by our great High Priest. We are exhorted to seize this hope as, in the hour of need, a sailor seizes the anchor-rope which is extended to him.

This is a development of what was in the writer's mind when he introduced the "great salvation" theme in chapters 1 and 2. There, he exhorts: "Therefore we must pay the closer attention to what we have heard, lest we drift away from it" (2:1). He was speaking to people who had already fled for refuge from their lost condition and found security in Jesus. So security is not now the issue. Here, as always throughout this epistle, the writer is looking beyond the place of refuge to "the hope set before us", which is something quite different.

Under the Law cities of refuge were provided to which certain offenders could flee and where they could live in safety from the hands of the avenger. But God has a better plan for us than that we should merely live securely in a city of refuge. Jesus has indeed provided security for those who believe in him, and for that we will be eternally grateful. But what of "the hope set before us"—the hope of the inheritance? According to our writer (6:19): "We have this as a sure and stedfast anchor of the soul, a hope that enters into the inner shrine behind the curtain, where Jesus has gone as a forerunner on our behalf . . ."

Let us be quite clear as to what he is saying. Our anchor is "sure and stedfast", but its rope has not been wound around us and firmly knotted, so that we have no option but to be drawn along by it to our destiny. It is an anchor, or to be more precise, an anchor-rope, which comes within our reach. It is our responsibility to seize it. Furthermore, we may do so with perfect confidence; in fact, with "strong encouragement", because we know that it is fastened firm and deep within the inner shrine or sanctuary of God's dwelling-place. That is not all, for we know also that within that inner shrine Jesus has entered "as a forerunner on our behalf, having become a high priest for ever after the order of Melchizedek".

"We have strong encouragement to seize the hope set before us." This is the word of the Lord to those who are truly his disciples; those who understand "salvation", not in the minimal terms of justification only, but in terms of the divine purpose that Jesus should bring many sons to glory. "He learned obedience through what he suffered; and . . . became the source of eternal salvation to all who obey him" (5:8,9). He has himself entered into the "inner shrine" as an overcomer, and as the pioneer (or file-leader) and guarantor of all those who, in the obedience of faith, have claimed his high priestly support, and follow him.

In Hebrews 11 our writer says further of Abraham that "when he was called to go out to a place which he was to receive as an inheritance . . . he went out, not knowing where he was to go". It was enough that Abraham had received God's call. Strong in faith "he looked forward to the city which has foundations whose builder and maker is God". We have this testimony also from Jesus that "Abraham rejoiced that he was to see my day; he saw it and was glad" (John 8:56).

God's men and women living in these perilous days need no more than his promised grace to walk confidently and gladly in the same pathway of faith. Just where, in the short term, that pathway may lead for each of us, is known only to him. For some, as for Abraham, it may involve a complete change of lifestyle. For others, outward circumstances may not change very much. But for all who hear the divine call, a "radical" transformation is inevitable; that is to say, a whole new change of purpose, of outlook, of motivation for living. We are the Lord's "called" people. To the exhortation: "Let us go on", there can be only one response: "YES, BY GOD'S GRACE, WE WILL!"

Postscript

Crisis in Grace Community Church

JIM FREEMAN WAS A CONVERT OF WHOM GRACE COMMUNITY Church was justly proud. Formerly, on his own confession, a philanderer, and a fiddler of his firm's books, it was, as he freely admitted, the fear of God that sobered him up.

An office colleague had persuaded him to attend a "guest meeting" at the church, and as the preacher spoke of God's judgment of sin, he had to listen. If there was a God and an after-life, Jim reflected, his prospects were pretty bleak, unless he mended his ways.

But how could he muster the necessary will-power to do that? Just as he was asking himself that question the preacher read a passage from the bible where it said that it is by grace you are saved, through faith, and it is not from yourselves, but is a gift of God; not of works, so that no-one can boast.

"I didn't understand it at first," Jim said, when he gave his testimony some months later at a crowded celebration event in the City Hall ". . . like so many adverts in the papers, it seemed too good to be true."

In response to the preacher's appeal, however, Jim decided to go forward to be counselled. "Do you believe it's for you?" his counsellor asked Jim, as he too spoke of the grace of God.

"How could I say 'No'" said Jim, "when I had everything to gain by saying 'Yes'?" And that's what he did. He told Laura (his wife), and his two teenage children about it, and now began attending meetings at Grace Community Church. After a few weeks, Laura and the children also started to come with him.

Jim soon became an avid student of the bible under the ministry of Frank Goodman, the pastor, who was a gifted teacher of "the doctrines of grace". Over against "Grace",

Frank explained, there was something called "Legalism". Not only are we saved by grace, but by grace we are set free from "the Law".

"I've found this second part of the 'grace message' more difficult to understand," Jim admitted, when giving his testimony. "As a sinner far from God, I knew that nothing but grace could meet my need. But, since I've become a Christian, I find sin is still a problem sometimes. Experiencing God's grace has been wonderful, but I can't say I've yet found how to get free from feelings of guilt when I do or think or say things which don't seem quite right for a Christian."

Coincidentally, soon after Jim had given this testimony, the pastor came out very strongly on the "grace" theme in one of his sermons. "You may think I overdo this," he said introducing his subject, "but I'm afraid some of you have not yet fully grasped this important truth. My friends, let me remind you that the foundation on which our faith is built is the grace of God. The apostle Paul says that we are justified freely by God's grace through the redemption which is in Christ Jesus. By grace we now stand before God and man clothed in the righteousness of Christ. Against that, the law has no claim. As Paul again says (in Romans 7) by our identification with Christ in his death and resurrection, we are no longer 'married' to that old schoolmaster, the Law, but to Jesus our Saviour and Lord. As we abide in him we bring forth fruit for his glory. Yes, my friends, it's all of pure grace."

"For further confirmation," continued Pastor Frank, "let us look again at that great statement of Paul's in Romans 5, verse 1: 'Therefore, since we are justified by faith, we have peace with God through our Lord Jesus Christ.' What does it mean to be justified? Justification is a legal term which means the exact opposite of condemnation. If someone is brought before a magistrate accused of some crime, what has to be decided is whether the accused is guilty or innocent. That's what the jury has to decide. And if they find him guilty then the magistrate's duty is to see he is suitably punished. But if the verdict is 'not guilty', the man in the dock is pronounced innocent—and he walks out of court a 'justified' man. So let me ask you again tonight—

those of you here who have received Christ as your Saviour —'Are you justified?'" (An enthusiastic response of "Yes!" came back from the congregation.) "Free from the Law?" "Yes!" came the answer again. "Say it again, as though you know it and mean it!"

"Yes!" came the answer once more, louder than ever.

"That's great!" said Pastor Frank, obviously encouraged. "All I ask of you then, is that when you leave this place tonight you do so with the same joyful conviction with which that man should have walked out of court after hearing the magistrate pronounce him 'not guilty'.

"A word of warning, though. Out there, you have an enemy, lurking in the shadows. His name is Satan. He's also known as 'the accuser of the brethren'. He's waiting around to 'get' you. And this is how. He'll try to insinuate into your mind the conviction that, for some reason or other, you are not as innocent as this Word declares you to be. You're the exception to the rule. Something must have gone wrong with the treatment in your particular case.

"When justified sinners allow thoughts of self-condemnation like that to capture their minds, and rob them of their peace and joy, it simply means that they've been playing into the hands of 'the accuser of the brethren'. When we do that we are like the foolish Galatians, to whom Paul wrote saying they had 'fallen from grace'. And when that happens, you may be sure the devil rubs his hands with glee. 'Here's another one of these "born again", "Spirit-filled" Christians we've tricked into falling from the grace of God' he says. 'Come on, my dear Wormwood, just keep on feeding him (or her) with regular doses of legalism, and it won't be long before he openly denies the faith, saying it doesn't work'."

Jim Freeman felt much encouraged as he left the meeting that evening, and on the way home he made a resolution that the next time the devil threatened him with feelings of self-condemnation, he would tell "the accuser" that he was a liar from the beginning. Jim Freeman was no longer under condemnation. Christ had set him free. Arriving home, he went straight into the lounge to share his pleasure with Laura, who was sitting watching the 'telly'.

"What do you think . . ." he began excitedly. To his

surprise Laura did not return his glance. Instead, he saw that her eyes were focused down towards the carpet. Looking down, he realized why. In his excitement, he had come in without wiping his shoes, and had trodden thick mud into the new carpet which had been laid only a few days before.

In his pre-Christian days, Jim would have apologized immediately for his thoughtlessness. It was on the tip of his tongue to do so now. Just in time, however, he realized that to do that would amount to an admission of guilt. A trifling incident, maybe, but wouldn't that be a lapse into the bondage of legalism—a victory for the devil, literally within minutes of having resolved never again to fall into his hands? Jim looked lovingly at Laura. She was a good wife, but as yet she was quite immature spiritually and had little understanding of the truth about "grace". What could he say to her without compromising the truth?

"Well?" she muttered bleakly, as he paused to find the right words.

Jim took a deep breath. Then out it came. "You lie, Satan" he said vehemently, shaking his fist in the direction of the carpet. "I'd have you know I'm justified! Christ has set me free!"

For a whole long minute, Laura sat speechless. Then, rising from her chair, she walked out of the room, slamming the door behind her.

It took Jim several minutes to recover from the shock caused by Laura's dramatic reaction. What should he do now? It did seem that it was his husbandly duty to go after Laura, put his arm round her and assure her of his love for her, and then to try to explain the truth to her as simply as possible. But first, perhaps it would be as well to take off his muddy shoes and get into slippers, and sweep the worst of the mud off the carpet. Having attended to these preliminaries he found Laura in the office. As he entered, she was replacing the telephone receiver. "Somebody wanting me?" he enquired. "No", Laura replied, "I've rung your pastor".

"What about?" he asked her sheepishly.

"You'll know when he comes tomorrow evening," was the reply.

Jim's suspicions as to the reason for Frank Goodman's intended visit were fully confirmed when he arrived the following evening. Beginning with the incident of the muddy shoes, Laura went on to relate several other incidents which had happened during the last few months in which, in her opinion, Jim had behaved badly. "I'm probably no better myself," she admitted, "but at least I'm prepared to admit it. What's so hurtful is that, when I do say 'sorry', Jim looks at me as though even that is wrong."

Frank Goodman looked at Laura sympathetically.

"This is very sad," he said.

Jim nodded.

"Well, Jim?" prompted the pastor, as Jim offered no comment.

Jim cleared his throat. "Laura doesn't quite grasp it yet," he said, cryptically.

"Grasp what?"

"The doctrine of grace," explained Jim.

Laura's eyes began to flash warning signals.

"Jim," said the visitor, realizing that he must now take things firmly into his hands, "this is no way for you to be treating Laura. Surely you realize that the least you can do is to apologize?"

"Apologize?" exclaimed Jim with astonishment. "Are you encouraging me to fall from grace?"

Jim's question started off a wide-ranging theological discussion. In this he revealed his considerable grasp of the teaching he had received under Frank's ministry. But, to his further astonishment, Frank, with his greater knowledge of scripture, was able to bring text after text to support his contention that Jim had indeed been at fault, and ought to admit it, and say 'sorry' to Laura. It seemed nothing short of a denial of all that teaching of Frank's about "justification"—even as recently as in last night's sermon.

He told Frank so. "Jim," the pastor replied gently, "you're a great chap; and we all love you. I'm personally thrilled at the grasp you've got of the truth about the grace of God. But have you ever heard me say a Christian oughtn't to say sorry when he's done something that's hurtful to somebody else?"

"No," Jim agreed. "But then I don't recall that you've ever

touched on that sort of problem at all, except when you're preaching to unbelievers, which is hardly surprising really, since I can't see how the situation could arise for 'justified' sinners."

Frank looked a trifle embarrassed. "Why not, Jim?" he enquired.

"Because you've pointed out to us from the teaching of Paul in Romans and Galatians that we have been declared innocent, and that if now we have any feelings of guilt they come from the devil who is the accuser of the brethren."

Frank's face coloured slightly. "But surely, Jim, you realize that you were careless when you trod mud into the carpet like that. Not that it was a heinous sin, but it was rather careless, wasn't it? It wouldn't have cost you much to have said 'sorry' to Laura, surely?"

Jim nodded. "I was tempted to do just that, Frank. But just in time, remembering the terrific message of encouragement you had given us less than an hour before, I realized from whence that prompting must have come—from the accuser of the brethren."

At this point, when the conversation between the two men appeared to have reached an impasse, Frank Goodman rose to leave, and did so after shaking Laura's hand, and giving Jim a brotherly bear-hug. Only Laura, who had been a silent listener to the men's discussion, was convinced that anything useful had come out of the pastor's visit, and her subsequent references to him were distinctly more favourable than previously.

On the following Sunday morning, at the meeting of the church, testimony time proved exceptionally lively. Several people spoke of having experienced "a fresh touch of grace" following the Wednesday evening meeting. To the surprise of many, however, Jim Freeman sat tight.

Particularly appreciated was the testimony of a fairly recent convert named Phil. "I don't come to these meetings out of a sense of duty, but because I want to come," he said cheerfully amidst a chorus of "Amen" and "That's right" from the congregation. When the chorus had subsided, he added, "And when I no longer feel like coming, I'll stay away".

Crisis in Grace Community Church 89

"And that makes sense," thought Jim as he reflected later on Phil's testimony.

Frank's visit to the Freeman's home had left Jim confused. Since God is not the author of confusion, Jim decided that for the time being he would stick to the message of grace as he and young Phil understood it, and leave all that business about "saying sorry" until he could make out how it fitted with "the grace message"; if in fact it did.

Next Sunday morning as the Freeman family were having breakfast the sun was shining brightly through the window.

"Lovely day for a trip into the country," said Jim, looking out of the window.

Laura and the two teenagers looked delighted. "I'll pack a picnic, and we'll get away straight after the meeting," said Laura.

"But the meeting does drag on a bit sometimes," said Jim. "How about skipping it today, and getting off to the Common when we've cleared up here?"

The Freeman family had a most enjoyable day in the country; the highlight for Jim and son Pete being when they landed right in the middle of a stock car racing event. This had been a favourite pastime of Jim's in his pre-Christian days, and young Pete too had been getting interested. To add to their pleasure, Jim met several old friends, and the welcome they gave him and the family was almost as hearty as anything they could have hoped for if they had gone to G.C.C that morning.

On the following Sunday, as the forecast was for heavy rain, the family raised no objection to Jim's suggestion that they go to the meeting. Pete did, however, mention that there was a programme on TV which should be interesting, but it didn't finish until 11 o'clock. "No problem," said Jim cheerfully, "if we get away immediately it's over, we'd get to the meeting near the end of all that singing—just in time for the ministry."

So that's what the Freemans did. After the meeting, several friends made tactful enquiries as to whether they had had some problem with the car that morning, and as to why they had been missing last Sunday? Jim answered everyone quite honestly. They hadn't come last week because they had fancied a picnic in the country, and this morning they were late because they had wanted to see a programme on TV.

On hearing these explanations, Frank Goodman couldn't have been more tactful and kind. But Jim could see he had taken it rather badly, and he felt really sorry about that because he had a high regard for his pastor. Incredibly, it was young Phil who proved most unsympathetic. "You of all people, Jim," he said, when Jim told him about the picnic. "How could you do such a thing?"

Jim reminded Phil of his recent testimony in which he had declared that he came to church because he wanted to, and when he no longer wanted to come, he wouldn't. "But, of course, I knew that day would never come," the young man said confidently.

Jim smiled. "I'd have said that myself, a few months ago," he said.

Back in his home later, Frank Goodman discussed the problem of Jim Freeman with his wife Jane.

"What particularly bothers me is how Jim's new phase may influence some of the young folk in the fellowship. Jim's very popular with them. Some may see him as a model to be copied, especially as he can make out such a good case for his behaviour on the basis of his interpretation of the message of grace."

"Young Phil's recent testimony won't help much either," added Jane.

Frank Goodman saw this as something of a crisis situation in Grace Community Church, and decided that it must be discussed with his personal counsellor Calvin Strong.

"See this as a problem of life rather than of death," advised brother Calv encouragingly, as the matter was discussed on the phone. "Whatever you do, Frank, don't let it tempt you to give up on the message of grace. Go on loving Jim. Drop in to see him and his family as often as you can. Have them round for a meal. Ask Jim to take you to one of his stock car racing events. With faith and patience—you see—he and the family will soon be keener than ever."

Crisis in Grace Community Church

Frank Goodman did his best to carry out his friend's advice, and the Freemans obviously appreciated the kindness he and Jane showed them. But their attendance at church continued to be spasmodic and dilatory. And, as Frank had feared, there was also a noticable increase in slackness generally in the church. Even at the prayer meetings, attendances, which had never been particularly good, dropped still further. So did the collections.

One Sunday as Frank and Jane were on their way home after a particularly ragged meeting, they discussed what could be done to improve the situation. "Calv's insistence that I go on preaching 'grace' must obviously be respected," said Frank.

"I suppose so," said Jane, but without enthusiasm. "But I do sometimes wonder whether a strong dose of 'law' mightn't do some of the fellowship any harm."

Frank looked at her anxiously. "Better keep that to yourself, love," he said. "I don't think that would go down too well in a certain quarter."

"You mean Calv?" enquired Jane. Frank nodded.

That afternoon Mary Brown came to tea. Mary was one of the few older people in the fellowship, and was a saintly soul respected by all. She knew her Bible well, and the only snag in that connection was that she was reputed to be somewhat "arminian" in her views, though when someone asked her if this were true, she confessed she didn't know what "arminian" meant. On enquiry, however, she learned that it had something to do with the fact that she sometimes expressed convictions considered to be inconsistent with the "grace message" which was regarded as an essential feature of the church's life and ministry. Nevertheless, Mary was herself such a gracious, godly person, everybody agreed that her life spoke of Christ. As was to be expected of somebody as disciplined as Mary, it was unthinkable that she would arrive late to meetings unless through unavoidable circumstances. She was a regular supporter of the prayer meeting, and although far from well off, she was known to be, in a quiet way, very generous. And nobody in the church was keener to witness for the Lord than she.

"There's something on your mind, Mary?" suggested

Frank discerningly, as they sat in the lounge after tea.

"Well yes, brother," said Mary. "It's about this teaching on 'grace'".

"Anything wrong?" enquired Frank, as Mary fetched her Bible out of her handbag.

"Nobody has more cause to be thankful for the grace of God than I," said Mary. "I would be lost without it. For more than fifty years it's been my strength and stay."

"Carry on, Mary," said Frank, as Mary paused to find words.

"But Frank, the gospel is not only about the grace of God, is it?"

"Perhaps not, Mary; but it's the foundation of the gospel, surely?"

After a further pause, Mary replied, somewhat hesitantly.

"No Frank, to be truthful, I don't think it is. You've given us a lot of teaching from Romans lately, and as I've been looking again at those opening chapters, I've been struck by Paul's statement there that he's not ashamed of the gospel of Christ because 'therein the righteousness of God is revealed'. I would have thought that was the foundation of the gospel—the righteousness of God."

"Well Mary," said Frank, nodding cautiously, "in a sense you're right, of course. But, never let us forget that it's through the grace of God alone that the righteousness of God is imputed to us by faith."

Mary smiled. "Yes, Frank; that's a great and glorious foundational truth. I rejoice in it. But it's not the whole gospel, is it?"

"I'm listening, Mary," said Frank, as Mary turned over the pages of her Bible to the gospel of Matthew.

"You recently gave us a very helpful talk on the Beatitudes," said Mary. "You pointed out that it is the meek who will inherit the earth; those who hunger and thirst after righteousness who will be filled; the pure in heart who will see God."

"Well, Mary?"

"Well, Frank . . . I'm not always meek; nor do I always hunger and thirst after righteousness. And I have to confess I am not always pure in heart."

"But Mary," said Frank, "I'm sure you, of all people, want God's best for your life. We all slip up occasionally. From what I know of Mary Brown she's pretty quick to settle her accounts with her Lord."

"Maybe, brother; but it's not always been that way with me. After I was converted as a teenager I went through a very bad patch of backsliding."

Frank Goodman looked lovingly at his respected friend. "And it was the grace of God that restored you, Mary?"

"Yes, it was indeed . . . . But it didn't all happen in five minutes. The Lord had to have deep dealings with my heart before I came again into real peace. It was a very painful experience at the time. But how thankful I have been ever since for it!"

"My dear sister," Frank said hesitantly, "far be it from me to contradict someone who has been so much longer in the faith than I, but are you sure it was the Lord who made you go through that dark experience? If you had known then what you know now about the greatness and the availability of God's grace, don't you think you would have been set free more quickly?"

Mary shook her head firmly. "You think it might have been the devil who was responsible for that experience, brother?"

"I just wondered," replied Frank.

"No, Frank." said Mary emphatically. "By the fruits of that experience alone, I know it was not the devil's work. What he'd been telling me before that time was that my indulgence of the flesh was not sin at all. Why shouldn't I have my fling, and enjoy myself like everybody else, while I was still young? That dark experience led me to discover —what I had only faintly realized in the first flush of joy when I first came to the Lord—how deadly sin is, and how greatly the Lord must have loved me to die for me in order to set me free from its dominion. No, Frank, I wouldn't have missed that experience for anything. Without it, I doubt if I would ever have understood and appreciated the parable of the Prodigal Son in the way I do."

Pastor Frank nodded approvingly in the direction of his wife Jane who had been listening silently to the conversation. "So what particularly have you in mind to say to me now, Mary?" he asked.

"Just this, my friends," said Mary, turning first to Jane, and then to Frank. "In our Fellowship we have a lovely bunch of young people, and, to be honest, I don't know another church in the city which is reaching the young for Christ so successfully as Grace Community Church. We've got life, and we've got love, and a pastor and his wife who really care. But those things are not enough. What I'm afraid of is that, unless these young folk are really taught about the exceeding sinfulness of sin, and what it really means to be a disciple of the Lord, many of them will lose their way."

"I think I know what you mean, Mary. Jane and I are not blind to these problems, I assure you. But what more can we do than go on presenting the grace of God to them? One has only got to look at the state of Christendom as a whole to realize how deadly it is to hammer away at people with the old legalistic 'thou shalt- thou shalt not- type of preaching'. But perhaps you don't agree?"

Mary smiled. "That would be swinging to the opposite extreme, brother," she said. "What is needed today, I believe, is that we do, as Paul claimed he had been doing during those years when he was ministering in Ephesus."

Mary fingered the pages of her Bible and opening it at Acts 20, read: "And now, behold, I know that all you among whom I have gone preaching the kingdom will see my face no more. Therefore I testify to you this day that I am innocent of the blood of all of you, for I did not shrink from declaring to you the whole counsel of God."

"And you are saying, Mary, that Frank is not doing that?" asked Jane, anxiously.

Mary looked at Frank. "Do you want my honest opinion on that?" she asked him.

"Of course, Mary. We have the greatest respect for you, and value your judgment very highly."

"Then I will give it," replied Mary, closing her Bible. "In my opinion you are not presenting the gospel of Christ in its fulness. In your eagerness to get as far away as possible from what you call legalism, and to emphasize the truth about the grace of God, you are missing out in your ministry some essential ingredients of the Gospel of the Kingdom, which Jesus preached and which he commanded his disciples to preach to the nations."

"Such as . . .?" Frank asked.

"The warnings which Jesus, and the apostles—including Paul—gave, not only to the unbelievers, but to the believers also, concerning sin and its consequences. You love Paul's epistle to the Romans, I know. But in that epistle Paul not only tells us about the grace of God which provides those who believe with the 'imputed' righteousness of Christ; he also looks at the tragic possibility of a believer 'continuing in sin'. Look at what he says here in the sixth chapter, verse 12: 'Let not sin therefore reign in your mortal bodies, to make you obey their passions. Do not yield your members to sin as instruments of wickedness, but yield yourselves to God.' Look at the warnings Paul gives in his epistles to the Corinthians. 'You are God's temple, and the Spirit of God dwells in you,' he says in the third chapter of the first epistle; and then goes on to say, 'If any one destroys God's temple, God will destroy him.'"

"What do you think that means, Mary?" asked Jane.

"I don't exactly know," admitted Mary. "But I do know that those words were addressed to Christians, and they must mean something. And that is not an isolated example of a warning to believers. I find them right through the New Testament from Matthew to Revelation."

"All right, Mary. Point taken. So what do you want me to do?"

"I want you to go on preaching the grace of God, as Paul said he did in Ephesus. But I beg of you to preach it in the context of the whole counsel of God, as Paul did. The Sermon on the Mount, which is the first recorded sermon in the New Testament, is not all about the Beatitudes. There are warnings in it too; and they were intended for the ears of the disciples primarily, as Matthew clearly shows. The same goes for all the later teaching of the Lord. Frank, you are doing a grave disservice to young converts to Christ when you tell them, regardless of whether they are 'continuing in sin', on the assumption that, in spite of everything, 'grace will abound', that they are 'innocent', and that if they allow any feelings of guilt to arise in their hearts it means they have become ensnared by legalism."

Mary's admonition obviously shook Frank, though she noticed that Jane's head appeared to be cautiously nodding in agreement.

"Well, Mary, to get down to the practicalities," said Frank. "Have you any evidence that assumptions of that kind are being made by any people in the Fellowship?"

Mary nodded. "Yes, Frank, I'm afraid I have."

"Would it be betraying any confidences if you mention any of them to us?"

"I think you know some of them already, brother. Jim Freeman tells me that his changed attitude with regard to his involvement in the Fellowship is the fruit of a better understanding of your teaching about the grace of God. And then there's young Phil."

"What about Phil?" asked Frank anxiously.

"Well, brother, if you don't know, it is not being sneaky to tell you, because he doesn't mind who knows. You know he has a girl friend, of course?"

Frank nodded. "Yes, that lass who came along to his baptism. What about her?

"They're sharing a flat together."

"But, Mary; I understood he'd decided to give that up?"

"So did I," said Mary. "But when I met him in the street this morning, he told me he'd changed his mind."

"Did he give his reason, Mary?"

Mary nodded. "Yes, very definitely. He said that after reading his Bible at the time of his baptism he had decided that it was wrong for a Christian to indulge in sex outside of marriage, and as a consequence, he had been feeling guilty ever since about his present life-style, until you gave that message about being free from the law. That changed his mind. Since then, after talking things over with Jim Freeman, he says he feels perfectly free to carry on living with the girl, and, as an added encouragement, he tells me that she's now promised to come with him to the Fellowship."

Frank was obviously in some distress as he glanced at Jane. "So what do we do now?" he pleaded.

Mary came up with an answer. "I suggest we three seek the Lord now to help us all to be more attentive to his word, and ask him to help us to be faithful as Paul was in declaring it in all its parts—'without fear or favour'—as my old pastor used to say. Could we do that now?"

Frank nodded agreement, and he was the first to pray. Mary and Jane followed.

A few minutes later, Mary said she should leave.

"What now?" Jane asked Frank when Mary had left.

"I think I'll ring Calv," said Frank.

Jane smiled wearily. "That'll be an expensive call, I'm thinking," she said. "But carry on; and if you don't mind, I'll listen on the other line".

Frank dialled Calvin Strong's number.

"Hullo, Myrna," he said, when the familiar voice of Calvin's wife answered his call. "Frank Goodman here. Is Calv around? There's something rather urgent I want to talk to him about."

"Sorry, Frank. I'm afraid you've just missed him. He's just left for Heathrow. Something rather serious has blown up in one of the big fellowships in Canada. But, if all goes according to plan, he should be back in three or four days. I'll make a note to let him know you want to speak to him. Sorry I can't be more helpful."

Frank replaced the receiver.

"I guess I'd better take a day or two off to think things over. Maybe there's some truth in what dear Mary has been saying."

Jane nodded. "A lot, in my opinion," she said.